Preface		
Decade One	**1923-1932**	**7**

My family and growing up with polio in the great depression • School play at St. Patrick's • Duke Slater

Decade Two	**1933-1942**	**13**

Ozzie Simmons • Time Goes By • Playing Sports • My Favorite Sport • Nile Kinnick

Decade Three	**1943-1952**	**21**

Dave Danner • Jim Sangster • Emlen Tunnell • Bruce Smith • Mom in Chicago • Parley cards • Wally Ris • Al Grady article
Murray Weir • Pops Harrison • How Louise and I met • Working at Bremers • Dick and Ralph Woodard • Herb & Scott Thompson

Decade Four	**1953-1962**	**45**

The Evy Era Coaches • Evy and Jim Milani • The Fainting Irish • Randy Duncan • Forest Evashevski
Joe Murphy & Hawkeye Players • Simon Estes • Bucky O'Connor • Don Norton • Bob Jeter • The Spelling Bee
Wilburn Hollis • Jim Evashevski and Clyde Bean

Decade Five	**1963-1972**	**57**

The Amana VIP • Jerry Burns • Paul Krause • Lloyd Berger • Trip to Hong Kong • Louise on TV
Francis X Cretzmeyer • The Six Pack

Decade Six	**1973-1982**	**69**

Johnson County I-Club • Alex Karras • I-Club Presidents • Disneyland with the Girls • Dave Triplett • Bobby Elliott
Ed Rate Poem • John Harty • Mike Gatens • Town Hawks • Andre Tippett • Carver-Hawkeye Fundraiser • Tim Riley
Jim Hayes • John Alt • T-Shirts and the NCAA • Bump Elliott and Bobby Knight • Pink Paint Job
Taffy Apple Murphy • Herky History • Tiger Hawk History • America Needs Farmers

Decade Seven	**1983-1992**	**91**

Iowa Honorary Letterman • Lute Olson • George Raveling • 1985 Football • Barry Alvarez • Introducing Hayden • Bill Quinby
Sports Opinion • Rotary Response • 1987 Holiday Bowl • Jimmy Rodgers • Garden Club • The Hawk Sculpture, the Street,
and the Scholarship for Bump Elliott • Chris Street Memorial • Floyd of Rosedale • Bob Downer • Wayne Duke

Decade Eight	**1993-2002**	**117**

Mount Rushmore • Irving Weber • Dan Gable • Tim Dwight • Shooting on Campus
We had seen enough! • One of a Kind • Irving Weber • Trip to Hawaii

Decade Nine	**2003-2012**	**127**

Scholarship • Tony Moeaki Touchdown • Jets Flyover Kinnick • What my Children Remember • The Swarm

Decade Ten	**2013-2016**	**141**

John Streif • Smiley • Mark Wilson • Ted Pacha • Fun at Football Games • Doug Goodfellow • Megan Blank
Wrestling at Kinnick • Longevity of Coaches and Administrators • Bob Brooks • Fred Mims • Renewed Vows
I Just Love Iowa Football • Epic Birthdays • Kirk Ferentz • New Football Facility • God Bless Us, Everyone

PREFACE

Murph Murphy: a 'Hawk' for all seasons

al grady

Article written in 1976 for the Iowa City Press Citizen

Earle Murphy makes no claims as to being the University of Iowa's No. 1 sports fan, or any such titles, but if there is a more ardent booster, faithful follower or dependable contributor to the Hawkeye cause than "Murph," he would be hard to find.

Murphy, a life-long Iowa Citian and the president of Bremers Inc., recently was saluted by the statewide I-Club, which helps support University of Iowa athletics, as its "man of the year."

The choice was not surprising and, in fact, may have been a bit overdue.

"A young 52" (by his own admission), Murph already has seen every Iowa football game this fall, having been drenched at Syracuse, toasted at Ohio State and drizzled at Indiana, in addition to watching the "sunshine games" in Iowa City.

Will he be at the Homecoming game Saturday?

(Is Murphy Irish?)

Of course he will, as well as at Northwestern next week, etc. He plans to see 'em all this season, night or day, home or away.

But that's not unusual for Murph, who became a "Hawk" at age five or thereabouts and can be seen at almost any Iowa track meet or basketball game or wrestling meet or baseball game or pep rally or you name it.

* * *

OVER THE YEARS, because he's worked at Bremers for almost 30 years, and because Bremers is a men's clothing store in the center of downtown, Murph has become acquainted with and befriended literally hundreds of Iowa athletes in all sports.

Ask any Iowa athlete of the last 30 years to name some of the persons he remembers best from his days on campus and the name "Murph Murphy" will be near the top of the list.

Murph contacted polio (then called infantile paralysis) in 1929 at age six, which left him with a limp, but one which is hardly visible today. Despite the handicap, he played basketball for the old St. Patrick's High School under coach Cliff Kritta as a sophomore, junior and senior.

He recalls seeing his first Iowa football game "about 1936" and also recalls tossing the football around with such early Iowa heroes as Ozzie Simmons and Homer Harris when they lived next door at the rooming house for black athletes on South Dubuque Street.

* * *

"I CAN'T REALLY RECALL when I first went to an Iowa game," says Murph, "but I really began to get interested when Nile Kinnick and the Ironmen came along. I sure remember the day they beat Minnesota 13-9, and the week before that when they beat Notre Dame 7-6.

"You know, one of the things I kind of miss in today's football is that there's no such thing as a triple-threat back anymore. Kinnick, you know, not only ran and passed, but he also did the punting and drop-kicked extra points. It was fun to go early to the pre-game warmups in those days and watch a guy like Kinnick practice his specialties. We used to go early, I remember, and watch Dick Crayne, who was one of the best punters Iowa ever had."

Murph graduated from St. Pat's in 1943 and attended Iowa for two years before a frequent fellow passenger on the morning bus route, Harold Reedquist, asked him one day, "How'd you like to go to work at Bremers?"

Murph said "okay" and hasn't changed his mind since. After the store was gutted by fire in 1963, Murph bought part ownership in the business and later became president.

* * *

IN THE MEANTIME, on Sept. 29, 1950, he met the former Louise Barnes of Washington, Iowa, who had just completed her nurses' training at Mercy Hospital here. Murph says he remembers the exact date of their "first date," because they went to a City High football game, then went home and listened to the Iowa-USC game from Los Angeles (which Iowa won 20-14).

Louise has become just as avid a Hawkeye fan as Murph, perhaps for self-preservation. Louise and Earle were married in 1951, and the couple has seven children. Oldest daughter Ann arrived home earlier this week for a two weeks "Homecoming" visit from Alaska and oldest son Jim attends the university and works part-time at Bremers. After that come Joe and John and Jeff and Jerry and Mary Sue.

It's a whole houseful of Hawkeye fans and a highlight of the Homecoming weekend is the post-game party at the Murphy's. Actually, not ALL Iowa fans are invited — it just seems like that.

Murph has seen Iowa play football at each of the other Big Ten stadiums on several occasions and also at the Los Angeles Coliseum, but one thrill has escaped him to date — watching Iowa play in the Rose Bowl. On Iowa's two previous appearances, after the 1956 and 1958 seasons, Murph had to work and couldn't make it.

* * *

HIS TALK OF Hawkeye highlights includes "beating Ohio State 6-0 in 1956 and Alex Karras knocking that guy down on the last play of the game . . . beating Notre Dame 48-8 that same season . . . that game we lost 38-28 to Ohio State in 1958, that was a great one even if we did lose . . . that Saturday afternoon basketball game for the Big Ten championship with Illinois in 1956 . . . those great days of Murray Wier in basketball. . . .

"It was so much fun to watch (the late) Emlen Tunnell play football and I was fortunate that Tunnell became a real close friend and one of my favorite persons . . . watching Willie Fleming play was always a great thrill, and Alex Karras and Jim Gibbons and a whole lot of others. I still think Larry Lawrence would have been the best quarterback Iowa ever had if he hadn't got caught in a 'political' situation. . ."

Murphy, who's a past-president of the Johnson County I-Club and one of the "Town Hawks," organized by Bob Commings to help recruits and their parents visit the university, says he believes "there never has been a better feeling than right now between the coaches and the athletic director."

HE'S A STRONG BACKER of Coach Commings and comments:

"When Commings made his tour through Iowa a couple of years ago in an effort to get the job, like a lot of other people, I wasn't much turned on at first. It probably wasn't very realistic, but I wanted a 'name coach' like Woody Hayes or Ara Parseghian or somebody.

"But after I heard him talk at a meeting here when he was campaigning, I was very much impressed and I keep getting more impressed all the time. I think if the fans of Iowa can have some patience with Bob, we are going to have many happy days in that stadium across the river.

"I think he is a great motivator and I think he knows the science of football. He's an excellent recruiter. The way he talks to recruits is with complete honesty. I talk to many of the players who drop into the store from time to time and they all have a lot of respect for him."

Then Murph says, somewhat with tongue in cheek, "The most important thing he's got going for him is that he's married to an Irishman named McGinnis."

To which daughter Ann replies, "That's not Irishman, dad, it's Irishperson."

To which Murph throws his head back and has a good laugh.

The Irish will not be divided in the Murphy household, nor will the "Hawks."

It's all for one and one for all.

FOREWORD

Behind the scenes, Earle "Murph" Murphy was always working for the benefit of the Iowa athletic department. I can't think of anyone who has been more of a friend, or more helpful to our administrators, coaches, and student athletes than Murph.

In his upstairs office at Bremers in downtown Iowa City, the coffee pot was always on and the conversation was usually geared towards Iowa sports. Before the internet, the place to go for Hawkeye gossip was Bremers.

Earle has been awarded many honors for his contributions and support of Iowa athletics. The National I-Club named him the "Hawk of the Year" in 1975, and the Iowa Varsity Club named him an honorary "Letterman" in 1984.

One achievement, and one for which I am most thankful, was his accomplishment in getting "The Hawk" sculpture to campus. Without his efforts, determination, and leadership the project would not have happened.

From his friendship with football star Ozzie Simmons in 1934, through his attending every home football game in 2014, Murph remains one of the most positive and passionate Iowa fans.

Enjoy these stories from his unique involvement with Iowa athletics as a local businessman, volunteer, and fan.

C.W. "Bump" Elliott
University of Iowa Director of Athletics
1970-1991

Dedication

I dedicate this book to my wife, Louise.
We have been married for 65 years. She worked beside me at Bremers. She cheered for the Hawks with me. She did much of the work raising our seven children Ann, Jim, Joe, John, Jeff, Jerry, and Mary Sue. She has taken great care of me.
Louise, thank you!

This book is also dedicated to the memory of Jack Shay.
We were great friends. In our weddings, we were each others Best Man.

My 92 years of life have been full and rewarding. I love Iowa City and the Hawkeyes. I hope you enjoy reading these stories as much as I've enjoyed living them.
Earle Murphy

Acknowledgments

Special thanks to Ann Murphy Pearson and John Murphy,
who put my memories into print. Without your efforts,
this book would have never been completed.

Thanks to Louise Murphy, Bonnie Murphy, all my children,
and the Briarwood Health Care Center staff,
for your patience and support of "The Book" project.

Thanks to Dawn Schindler, Bob Elliott, and Mark Wilson
for your assistance and guidance.

Thanks to Bob Goodfellow, the UI Athletics Department,
and Special Collections, University of Iowa Libraries,
for approval of photographs used in this book.

Thanks to Bill Bywater and Tru-Art Color Graphics
for publishing this book.

Book proceeds will be donated to the
Earle and Louise Murphy University of Iowa Athletic Scholarship Fund,
and Briarwood Health Care Center in Iowa City.

Iowa Stadium Dedication Game, October 19, 1929
Photo Courtesy of Special Collections, University of Iowa Libraries

Murph Remembers...

Decade One | 1923-1932

Murph Remembers...

Above: Back row: My parents Perry and Esther Murphy
Front row: My sister Lucile, myself, my sister Pauline

L-R Pauline, myself, Lucile.
Top right photo taken in 2016. Lower right photo taken in 1945.

Old Iowa Field was located directly east of the Iowa River, north of Burlington Street and south of Iowa Avenue. The framed picture was given to me by family friend Charles "Bud" Erickson. It was taken with a panoramic camera by a photographer working for the Hebard-Showers Company. On this day, November 15, 1913, Iowa beat Ames 45-7. If you look closely on the right side of the photo, you'll see people have climbed trees, telephone poles, and up onto the rooftops, to get a glimpse of the football game. I love this old photo.

"Murph remembers..."

Decade 1

Growing up with polio in the Great Depression

I was born in a farmhouse four miles south of Oxford, Iowa, on September 11, 1923. My parents were Perry and Esther Murphy. I have an older sister Lucile and a younger sister Pauline.

We moved to the rural east side of Iowa City when I was four years old. My Dad worked as a tenant farmer for numerous years until getting a job with the county working on the roads and bridges. My father also helped build Kinnick Stadium.

Mom plucked and cleaned chickens for a lady who raised them south of town. After that she worked in the kitchen at the University of Iowa Hospital. Her final job was working behind the counter at Plamor Lanes bowling alley downtown. She also made homemade pies for the customers.

In 1929, at the age of six, I was diagnosed with polio and sent to the University of Iowa Children's Hospital for treatment. My polio affected my right leg and foot, and I wore a brace until I had surgery when I was 11 years old.

We moved to a small house located at 714 S. Dubuque Street near downtown Iowa City, located next to the train tracks. As a young boy I would crawl up into the train cars and take pieces of coal which I could sell or we could use at home. In the early 1930's during the Great Depression, numerous men would ride the trains looking for work. They would jump off in Iowa City and knock on our door. We were poor but my Mom would feed them when possible.

Money was tight and times were tough in Iowa City and throughout the country. We could not afford the $14.00 a month rent, so we moved two blocks south to 912 S. Dubuque Street, where the rent was $12.00 a month.

One year during the depression, just before Christmas, my Dad went to the back yard and I heard a gunshot. He came back inside and exclaimed, I shot Santa Claus and there won't be any Christmas presents this year!

Yes, times were tough during the Great Depression.

Photo Courtesy of Special Collections, University of Iowa Libraries

Photo Courtesy of Special Collections, University of Iowa Libraries

Game at Iowa Field, circa 1917

Iowa Stadium Dedication Game, October 19, 1929

The School Play at St. Patrick's School
My Name is John

In 1931, when I was eight years old, I attended St. Patricks' School in Iowa City. At that time I'd had polio for two years. I wore a brace on my right leg from the knee down to keep my foot from curling under. Without the brace my toes would have curled under and touched my heel and I wouldn't have been able to walk.

Near the end of the school year, my third grade class put on a play called, "My Name is John!" It was performed in front of our friends and parents.

On the night of the performance this is what happened: One of the scenes of the play was about a car hitting a boy riding on a bicycle. All of the actors created a big commotion. One person yelled, "Somebody call a doctor!" Another student yelled, "John, you go because you're the fastest!" Well, I had the part of John. So, when I limped off the stage hurrying to find a doctor, the Irish crowd roared with laughter.

Remember… "It's better to limp all the way to heaven, than not get there at all".

> **Remember…**
> **"It's better to limp all the way to heaven, than not get there at all".**

Earle Murphy is top row, far left.

Myself, our dog Rex and my sister Pauline, circa 1932
In the backyard of our home at 912 S Dubuque St in Iowa City

Duke Slater
The first black All-American at Iowa

Frederick Wayman "Duke" Slater played football for Iowa from 1918-1921. He led Iowa to a perfect 7-0 record his senior season. He helped Iowa defeat Notre Dame, 10-7, which snapped a 20 game winning streak for their famous coach Knute Rockne. Slater excelled as a tackle on offense and defense, and was named to the All-Big Ten first-team three times. He was also a first-team All-American, making him the first black All-American athlete at Iowa. Duke Slater and Nile Kinnick were the only two Iowa players elected into the College Football Hall of Fame in its inaugural year of 1951.

As a boy, "Duke" somehow picked up the nickname of the family dog. At his high school in Clinton, Iowa, each football player needed to provide his own shoes and helmet. His family could not afford both, so they decided to only purchase shoes. His feet were so big they had to be special ordered from a store in Chicago. He played throughout high school and college without wearing a helmet for protection.

Legendary Michigan coach Fritz Crisler played against him in college and said, "Duke Slater was the best tackle I ever played against. I tried to block him throughout my college career but never once did I impede his progress to the ball carrier." Duke played professional football for ten years, and was the first African-American lineman in NFL history. Due to racism and color bans by several teams, from 1928 to 1933, only five Afircan-Americans played in the NFL. In 1929, Slater was the only black player in the league.

During his professional football career, he would return to Iowa City in the off-seasons, and earned his law degree in 1928. He moved to Chicago and became an assistant district attorney, and in 1948 he was elected a judge with the city's Municipal Court. In 1960, he became a member of the Chicago Superior Court, then the highest court in the city.

I was fortunate to meet Judge Duke Slater at an Iowa-Wisconsin football game in 1958. He was at the game with his good friend Ozzie Simmons, another former Hawkeye football star. Slater Hall dormitory on the University of Iowa campus is named in his honor.

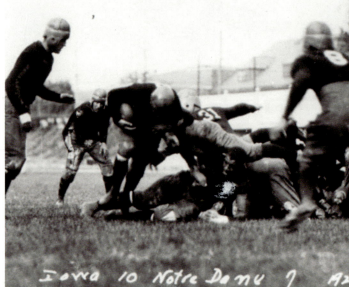

Photos Courtesy of Special Collections, University of Iowa Libraries

Duke Slater played high school and college football without wearing a helmet.

Murph Remembers...

Ozzie Simmons, the "Ebony Eel."

Decade Two | 1933-1942

Decade 2

"Murph remembers..."

Ozzie Simmons
My Childhood Friend and Hero

The year was 1934, and the Great Depression was well underway. Ozzie Simmons lived at 828 South Dubuque Street along with his brother, Don, and six other African American athletes. They all played football for Iowa. I lived nearby, at 912 South Dubuque Street with my mom, dad, and two sisters. In 1929, when I was six years old I was infected with the polio virus and was in and out of the University of Iowa Children's Hospital. I was 11 years old when I had my first operation on my foot and soon was back home in my neighborhood. I wanted to be active, but I had limitations due to the surgery.

When Ozzie found out that I was back living in the house, he asked my mom if he could carry me across the street to Kelly field. (This area is where the armory was later built.) My mom agreed and Ozzie would take me over and set me down on the field. They let me be their center. I had a great time centering the football for them! The players included: Iowa's captain, Homer Harris, Don Simmons and three others. They included me in about five of their private practice sessions. We all had a good time, and I felt really special getting to play with them; just think, little Earle Murphy, "a little crippled boy" playing with star Iowa football players! Ozzie treated me very well and also gave me a baseball, bat, and basketball.

> **"The way he took care of me was the beginning of my love of Iowa athletes and Iowa sporting events."**

Playing football games against Minnesota was a dangerous endeavor for African-Americans in the 1920's and 1930's. Jack Trice was Iowa State's first black football player. He died from injuries sustained in a game at Minnesota in 1922. He was kicked, punched, and trampled by several Minnesota players. Two days after the game, he died due to internal bleeding and hemorrhaged lungs. The football stadium in Ames is named Jack Trice Stadium in his honor.

Ozzie Simmons is probably best known as the central figure in the story of Floyd of Rosedale. Ozzie's first year playing for Iowa was in 1934. There were few black football players in the Big Ten in the early 1930's and Ozzie was unfairly targeted by the Minnesota defense during the Iowa - Minnesota game. He was injured during the first half by numerous 'piling on' at the end of plays, and knocked out. The referees never called any penalties on the offending players. His injuries kept him from returning for the second half.

The next year, before the Iowa - Minnesota game there were concerns about Ozzie being injured once again due to similar reoccurring problems. While talking to a reporter, Iowa's governor, Clyde Herring stated, "If the officials stand for any of the rough tactics like Minnesota used last year, I'm sure the crowd won't!" To try to defuse the situation, Minnesota's governor, Floyd B. Olson, made a wager with Iowa's governor. If Minnesota won the football game, then they would be awarded a prize pig. It just so happened that Minnesota did win in a clean and fair game. The governor of Iowa obtained a Hampshire hog from the Rosedale Farms near Fort Dodge, Iowa, and presented it to the Minnesota governor and fans after the game. The pig was named Floyd of Rosedale, after the governor of Minnesota and the farm it came from. After the original Floyd of Rosedale died, the Minnesota governor had a bronze pig made and Floyd of Rosedale trophy was born. Playing for the coveted Floyd of Rosedale trophy has become a tradition between Iowa and Minnesota every year.

Time Goes By

On October 18, 1958 I took my wife Louise and two of our children, Ann and Jim to Madison, Wisconsin, for the Iowa-Wisconsin football game. We had great seats in Camp Randall stadium. I was really surprised that there were two empty seats to my left. About five minutes into the game I looked up and saw two black gentlemen, who were very well dressed, coming towards me. They sat in the empty seats next to me. The man who was sitting next to me started asking me questions about the Iowa players and after a while I decided to introduce my family. He told me his name was Ozzie Simmons and his friend was Duke Slater.

I noticed my wife was catching her breath and quivering with excitement. I waited a couple minutes, tried to gain my composure, and said, "Ozzie do you remember that little crippled boy you carried across the street to Kelly field who acted as your center?"
Ozzie replied, "You're not that little crippled kid!"
I said, "Yes I am!"
He said to Duke Slater, "This is the little crippled kid that I talked about."
Ozzie wanted to know what I was doing and I told him about working at Bremers.

Ozzie and Duke visited with me throughout the game. Iowa went on to win that 1958 Wisconsin game and finished the football season with a trip to the 1959 Rose Bowl. Duke Slater was Iowa's first Black All American in 1921, and Slater Residence Hall on the UI campus is named in his honor.

I feel that running into Ozzie and Duke at the Madison game was a **miracle**!

Playing Sports

I would go swimming the Iowa River for my own personal style of physical therapy. There was no way we could afford the traditional type at a clinic, so I would swim in the river. Working against the current was great exercise. My mom never knew; I was sure she would have worried too much. I think swimming made my legs get stronger. I loved sports and by getting stronger I was able to play sports in school.

Earle

Softball

During WWII Gas Rationing

In 1942 there was no special transportation system set up for Iowa's Basketball team. So, Dean Jones, Earl Sangster, Roland Smith, Steve Brody, and Hugh Jennings would fill their cars with gas and haul the basketball team to out of town games. This was one way Iowa City boosters helped their Hawkeyes.

My favorite sport to play was basketball

I love to watch all Hawkeye sports, but I loved to play basketball. Even with my polio and weak legs, I was still able to participate in high school basketball. I played center for Saint Patrick's High School. I had a pretty good hook shot and was able to start several games. I recall at least two games where I was the leading scorer. Not too bad for a 5 foot 9 inch center.

My coach was Cliff Krita. He would put a figure eight wrap around my crippled leg before every practice and game. My good friends Dave Danner, Bill Sangster, and Bob Roth all went to City High, but they would come and watch me play.

One of the freshman players on the team was Don Joe Gatens. He was very talented and ended up playing college basketball at Notre Dame. Don's son Mike played for Iowa in the 1970's and his grandson Matt also played at Iowa. Matt ended his fantastic Hawkeye career as the 6th All-Time Leading Scorer in Iowa history. Matt is currently playing professional basketball in Europe.

St. Mary's Repeats Earlier Wins With Second Half Drive

By CLAIR MOSELY

The old St. Mary's jinx which has plagued St. Patrick's cagers for 13 starts was present again Thursday night as the Ramblers made it 14 games in a row through a last quarter surge at the basket which left the final score at, 27-24. The Irish were out in front all the way until a basket by George Seemuth, Rambler forward, tied the score, 23-23, after a minute of play in the last period.

Ramblers Rally

St. Mary's (27)	FG	FT	PF	TP
Seemuth, f (co-c)	2	0	3	4
Sweeney, f	3	0	0	6
Bright, c	1	2	4	4
Brogla, g	3	1	1	7
Smith, g (co-c)	3	0	3	6
Ivie, g	0	0	0	0
Totals	12	3	11	27

St. Patrick's (24)	FG	FT	PF	TP
Murphy, f	4	0	3	8
McLaughlin, f	2	2	2	6
Grady, f	0	3	2	3
R. Connell, c	1	1	4	3
Gatens, g	1	2	0	4
W. Connell, g (co-c)	0	0	2	0
Totals	8	8	14	24

Score by quarters:
St. Mary's 8 12 21 27
St. Patrick's 10 18 23 24

From then on in the Marians took over, with Sweeney and Brogla contributing to the winning margin. With ten seconds left in the game, Bob Connell, Irish center, fouled out of the game along with Rambler center, Keith Bright. Don Gatens made a Shamrock free throw with only four seconds left, but further Irish attempts at the basket were useless.

The score was 2-up and 8-up at stages in the first quarter with the Irish taking over the lead by a field goal by Don "Red" Gatens making it 10-8 as the period closed. Phil McLaughlin opened the second stanza by making the score 12-8, but the Ramblers added another basket before the Irish, led by Earl Murphy, started on a scoring spree which netted them the half-time advantage, 18-12.

Murphy was the man of the evening as he poured in four field goals for an eight-point high in scoring for both squads, to make his last game for the Irish one of the best of his career.

Red Gatens Has A Try

In the above picture, Red Gatens, St. Patrick's guard, lets loose a one handed push shot from in front of the basket as teammates Phil McLaughlin and Earl Murphy, No. 4, and Ramblers Bill Sweeney, in the far corner, Mel Smith, No. 12, and Don Brogla, No. 14, look at the flight of the ball with some concern. That is Keith Bright attempting to block the shot.

Nile Kinnick, Iowa's Heisman Trophy Winner

I was 16 years old when Nile Kinnick won the Heisman Trophy in 1939. I saw him play a few times, but never had the opportunity to meet him. I would go over to football practice and watch him practice his punting. He would work with Coach Frank Carideo, who was a two-time All-American quarterback at Notre Dame. They were both outstanding punters. I remember Carideo being able to punt the ball as accurately as most could pass it. In the 1937 football season, Kinnick led the nation in punting.

I would go to games in the 1939 with my friend, Bob Myers. I remember we once took a large paper bag full of popcorn we brought from home. I think we paid 10 cents to get into the game...and I know we ate way too much popcorn while we watched the game in the stadium.

I know academics were very important to Nile Kinnick, and that he was an excellent student and public speaker. I did end up getting to know several of his Ironmen teammates. Most of them thought that if he hadn't died in the war, he would have been a Governor, Senator, or even President.

Carl "Bud" Strub, a friend of mine from Iowa City, recently provided me with a copy of one of the last letters ever written by Nile Kinnick. The copy was given to him by Jim Swaner, of Iowa City, who received it from Steve McCollister.

Steve McCollister's father was John McCollister. John, his older brother Ed, and Nile, were all members of the Phi Kappa Psi fraternity at Iowa. Ed McCollister served as President of the fraternity, and assisted in recruiting Nile into membership. They became good friends, and Ed moved to New York City after graduation. When Nile went to New York City to accept the Heisman Trophy award, he stayed with Ed McCollister.

The recipient of the letter wished to stay anonymous, and I'm not sure to whom it was written. One thing I know is that it proclaims Kinnick's love for Iowa City. It's also very eerie and sad, knowing that this letter was written on May 31st, 1943, two days before he died, on June 2nd, 1943. The tragic news of Nile Kinnick's death would have been announced before this letter was delivered.

Nile Kinnick, accepting the Walter Camp Player of the Year award in 1939.

Photo Courtesy of Mark Wilson

NILE KINNICK LONGED FOR IOWA

Monday
May 31, 1943

Dear

Your welcome letter reached me last night here in this far away place of which I am permitted to tell you nothing. Carrier life is interesting and adventurous, but after a time it begins to drag. Word from you boosted my spirits no end.

Am so glad you could speak enthusiastically of your visit in Iowa City. That little town means so much to me — the scene of growth and development during vital years — joy and melancholy, struggle and triumph. It is almost like home. I love the people, the campus, the trees, everything about it. And it *is* beautiful in the spring. Ah, for those days of laughter and picnics when the grass was newly green and about a grab and a half high. I hope your friend showed you through the Union, the Fine Art Bldg, the Little Theatre of which we are so proud. And I hope you strolled off across the golf course just at twilight and felt the peace and quiet of an Iowa evening, just as I used to do.

Nile C. Kinnick
Ensign U.S.N.R.

THE LETTER ABOVE is one of the last written by Iowa's Ens. Nile Kinnick, who died tragically last June when his navy plane crashed into the sea. It was received by a friend of his in Des Moines who prefers to remain anonymous. The letter says: "Your welcome letter reached me last night here in this far away place of which I am permitted to tell you nothing. Carrier life is interesting and adventurous, but after a time it begins to drag ... Word from you boosted my spirits no end. Am so glad you could speak enthusiastically of your visit in Iowa City. That little town means so much to me— the scene of growth and development during vital years— joy and melancholy, struggle and triumph. It is almost like home. I love the people, the campus, the trees, everything about it. And it is beautiful in the spring. Ah, for those days of laughter and picnics when the grass was newly green and about a grab and a half high. I hope your friend showed you through the Union, the Fine Arts Bldg., the Little Theater of which we are so proud. And I hope you strolled off across the golf course just at twilight and felt the peace and quiet of an Iowa evening, just as I used to do."

NILE C. KINNICK

One of Nile Kinnick's final letters speaks to his love of Iowa City.
Written on May 31st, 1943, he died on June 2nd, 1943.

Photo Courtesy of Bill Bywater

In 1939, Iowa's offensive line leveled Notre Dame's defense in the most famous play of University of Iowa football history. On the two yard line with fourth down, Iowa made up a play in the huddle to protect Nile Kinnick's two broken ribs on his right side. He carried the ball in his left arm, protecting his right side, into the end zone standing up. Kinnick drop kicked the extra point...Iowa wins 7-6! It was the upset of the year assuring Nile Kinnick the Heisman Trophy. In 1972, the University of Iowa football field was named Nile Kinnick Stadium in his honor.

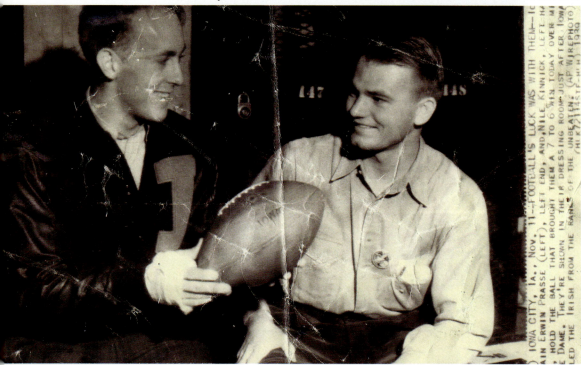

Locker room celebration after Iowa beats Notre Dame

Murph Remembers...

Street view of Bremers Clothing
Big crowd in the street in front of Bremers. I like the shot of the boy staring back at the camera.
I started working at Bremers in 1944.

Decade Three | 1943-1952

"Murph remembers..."

Dave Danner, City High and Iowa All-Around Athlete

Dave Danner was born in Iowa City and lived on Gilbert Street in the family apartment attached to John's Grocery, an Iowa City landmark.

He was a close friend and a talented and versatile athlete at Iowa City High in the 1940's. Dave was named First-Team All-State in basketball, Second-Team in football, and was a state champion in tennis.

His athletic career continued at Iowa as a basketball player, where he was named First-Team All-Big 10 in 1944. During the 1943-1944 basketball season, Iowa got off to a 12-0 start and ended up 2nd place in the Big Ten. In one game at Indiana, Iowa was behind by one point in the final minute when Dave stole an errant pass and scored the winning shot in the final seconds for a 43-42 victory.

Dave established the Herbert Cormack Scholarship in honor of his former coach and athletic director at City High. This scholarship has been awarded annually to a senior student at City High who exhibits academic promise and who plans on attending the University of Iowa.

Dave played competitive tennis into his 80's and was known to keep opponents off balance with his ambidexterity.

Herb Cormack and Dave Danner

Dean Jones, Murph, Dave Danner, Herb Cormack

Jim Sangster

Jim Sangster was "Mr. City High" for all that he did for the school. He was founder and President of the City High Alumni Association. Jim was all-state in football and basketball, and started on State Championship teams in both sports. He attended almost every game or event at City High for years. He was one of my best friends.

> **Jim Sangster was "Mr. City High" for all that he did for the school.**

City High State Champs 1946

as 25 years ago this week and these guys were happy—with good reason. They had just brought Iowa City High School its first, and only, state basketball championship, beating LeMars 41-40 when Bob Freeman made three baskets in the final 55 seconds of the most incredible finish in state basketball tourney history. Most members of the team and Coach Gil Wilson are meeting in Des Moines this weekend and are featured in the state tournament program. This is the way they looked then: Front (left to right), Bob Crowe, Bob Beals, Bob Krall, Bob Freeman, Bob Oldis (manager) and Gerri Cannon. Back row (left to right), Dale Stark, Jim Van Deusen, Gene Hettrick, Evan Smith, Coach Gil Wilson, Kirk Carson, Harry Dean Jr. and Jim Sangster.

(Press-Citizen Photo)

Murph Remembers...

Emlen Tunnell

Emlen Tunnell with Vince Lombardi

> "He was a man of many firsts: The first black man to play for the New York Giants. The first black man to be an assistant coach in the NFL. The first black man inducted into the NFL Hall of Fame!"

Eddie Anderson, Iowa's football coach in the 1940's used to like to shake hands with his football players. He had a very powerful grip and would enjoy shaking their hands so hard they would buckle down to their knees.

Dick Woodard had arranged a meeting with Emlen Tunnel to meet Eddie Anderson. Dick had forewarned Emlen about Eddie's forceful handshake habit, and Emlen was ready for him. Emlen grabbed Eddie's hand first and Eddie buckled. He just looked up at Emlen and buckled to his knees for the first time. Emlen had huge, strong and perfectly shaped hands

Emlen Tunnel played quarterback, halfback and defensive back during his two years at Iowa. In 1948, most pro teams thought Emlen would be returning to Iowa for his final year. He decided instead to pursue a pro career and approached the New York Giants, who eventually offered him a contract. Emlen played 11 years with the Giants and then finished up playing 3 years for Vince Lombardi and the Green Bay Packers.

In 1969, Lloyd Berger and I were in New York City on business and we found out there was a pre-season football game with the New York Giants playing the New York Jets.

The game was being held in New Haven, Connecticut and we decided to go. We took the train, and we had so much fun listening to the bantering back and forth between the Giant and Jet fans. It was really entertaining.

We did not have tickets so we waited for the Giants team bus to arrive. Emlen was an assistant coach at the time. I saw him get off the bus, yelled at him to get his attention, and held up my hand showing him we needed two tickets. He shouted back for us to stay by the bus. A few minutes later, a man came out, asked for Mr. Murphy, and gave us two tickets.

When Emlen was a scout for the Giants, he would come back to Iowa City for football games. One night around 10:30, Emlen called the house and asked me what I was doing. I said "I'm getting ready to go to bed." He asked if Louise and I wanted to meet him at the UI Athletic Club for a drink. I asked Louise and she agreed to go as she really liked Emlen. We had a nice time and I remember we were the last customers to leave the bar. Emlen would also come to our homecoming parties and entertain everyone with his stories.

Emlen may not be remembered as one of the all-time great Hawkeyes, but he had a fantastic pro career. He was a nine-time Pro-Bowl Selection. He excelled at punt returns, and played in 143 consecutive games.

He ended his career with an NFL record 79 interceptions (since surpassed by fellow Hawkeye Paul Krause).

He was a man of many firsts:
The first black man to play for the New York Giants. The first black man to be an assistant coach in the NFL. The first black man inducted into the NFL Hall of Fame!

In 1999, the Sporting News named The 100 Greatest NFL Football Players, and Emlen Tunnel was number 70 on the list.

During a practice session in 1975, while an assistant coach with the Giants, Emlen died from a heart attack at the young age of 50.

Emlen Tunnell was one of my All-Time Favorites!

Bruce Smith

He walks into Bremers, and tells the first salesman he sees that he wants to meet with me. Once he finds me he says, I'm Bruce Smith. I said, that sounds familiar. He said, I'm a Heisman Trophy winner. Bruce played running back for the Minnesota Gophers who were the national champions in 1940 and 1941. He received his Heisman Trophy two days after the attack on Pearl Harbor.

At the time he came to Bremers he was selling Rudoffer tuxes, and so we bought some tuxes and then we went to dinner together. There was a movie made about him, "Smith of Minnesota", exploiting his football talents and his All-American qualities. He married fashion model Gloria Bardeau, and they had four children. In 1967 at the age of 47, Bruce Smith died of cancer.

He was a wonderful person and a very religious man who some people thought should be canonized into sainthood.

My Mother and I Traveled to Chicago

When I was 25 years old, I took my mom to Chicago on the train. This was the first time she had ever been out of the state of Iowa. We went to the musical *Annie Get Your Gun*. Our hotel was the downtown Palmer House. It was a luxurious place to stay. Mom and I went to look out the window of her room to view the Chicago skyline. She simply looked at the drapes and noted how pretty they were. Seeing nice things, both a city view and the hotel furnishings all impressed her. I was really happy that I was able to treat my mom to this special trip.

Parley Cards

I went to a practice in 1947 and it seemed as though everyone had them. Coach Eddie Anderson asked what our odds were for the next game. I reached in my pocket to check the card. Eddie said, "Take that card and get out of here!"

The next morning, Eddie comes into Racine's Cigar Store and sits down next to me. I reach into my pocket and I said, "Purdue by 6."

Murph Remembers...
Wally Ris

Wally was a good friend and one of Iowa's greatest swimmers. He was a two time NCAA champion in 1948 and 1949. In the 1948 Olympics held in London, England, Wally won a Gold Medal in the 100 Meter Freestyle and a Gold medal in the 800 meter Freestyle Relay.

He told me that the Queen of England personally presented him his Olympic medals.

I remember one time he needed to go to Monticello and Anamosa for a swimming exhibition and he asked me if I would take him. I drove my '49 Olds Coupe. In later years he would send me pins from the different events he swam in from all over the world.

> **He told me that the Queen of England presented him his Olympic medals.**

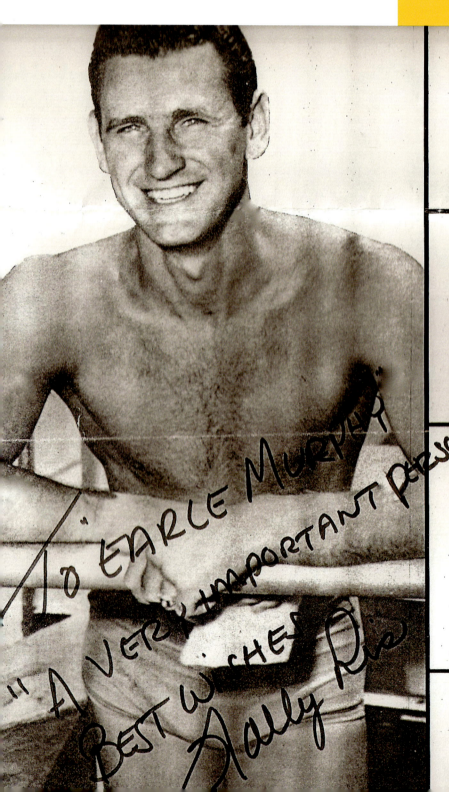

GOLD MEDAL 100 METER FREESTYLE
GOLD MEDAL 800 METER FREESTYLE RE

BIG TEN CONFERENCE

100 YARD; 220 YARD CHAMPION 1948
100 YARD CHAMPION 1949

N.C.A.A.

100 YARD CHAMPION 1948
100 YARD CHAMPION 1949
NCAA SWIMMER OF THE YEAR 1949

A.A.U.

Recalling the Glory Days of Pops Harrison

We've had a couple of items in the paper in the last few months about Pops Harrison being ill and in the hospital.

Normally, such items, when used, appear in the women's page, for some reason or another. And, the women's page editor, in such instances, insisted with great dignity and formality, that Pops Harrison must be referred to as Lawrence.

I argued, in vain, that no one would know who Lawrence Harrison was, anymore than anyone would know Yogi Berra by his given name of Lawrence.

Well, the women's page editor runs her page and I run mine and the managing editor tries to keep peace. So Pops Harrison appeared as Lawrence and I hope someone knew who he was.

Anyway, there will be a "gathering of the clan" tonight at the Harrison household and Pops surely couldn't have much better medicine than to see and visit with the many fine men who helped him write Iowa and Big Ten basketball history back in the 1940s.

The younger generation, or generations, couldn't possibly know what basketball hysteria was like in Iowa City back in those exciting, turbulent days during, and immediately after, World War II.

There has been much basketball excitement in this city for many years. There is now in the winter, during the coaching regime of Ralph Miller. And there was under Bucky O'Connor, too, back in the days of the Fabulous Five.

* * *

BUT I DON'T THINK BASKETBALL FEVER ever reached the pitch, before or since, that it did in those days from about 1944 through 1948, when Pops Harrison and his boys became household words across the Hawkeye state.

There was only one championship, in 1944-45, but there were a couple of near misses (second place in 1944 and 1948) and Pops' teams were almost always in the running for the Big Ten title and every game seemed like a life-or-death matter.

You've got to remember that this was eight or 10 years B.E. (Before Evashevski) and Iowa usually hadn't much to cheer about in football, and basketball was king.

Bill Porter, then a professor in the school of journalism, authored an article in the Saturday Evening Post called "Hoop Happy Town," in which Iowa City was extolled as the center of basketball madness. And he was right.

There were no "hippies" then, but everyone was hep, and the enthusiasm of the students for the basketball team bordered on the fanatic. The crowds were boisterous and wild and unruly.

WHEN THE HAWKEYES CLINCHED the championship in 1945 by beating Illinois to atone for their only loss of the season, some 3,000 fans herded onto the floor to congratulate Pops and his champs and it took them about 20 minutes to get to the dressing room.

I remember a night in February of 1948 when Wisconsin played here and the student mob could hardly wait. I was among those 5,000 waiting outside the fieldhouse for the doors to be opened at 5:30 p.m. and my feet are still cold! Can you imagine today's students waiting in line at 5 o'clock for an 8 o'clock game? Not many, I can't.

Well, Pops Harrison had a flair for life and a flair for coaching and "his boys" were just that. His sideline emotions, and his run-ins with officials, ranked with the very best. The Iowa mob loved Pops Harrison and they loved his players.

Most of all, they loved a red-haired runt from Muscatine named Murray Wier who appeared on the scene as a freshman in the title-winning season of 1945 and stayed for four glorious seasons.

* * *

WIER WAS ONLY 5-8 AND EVEN in those days he looked like a midget on the basketball court, but man, how he could shoot a basketball! He never quite learned the art of making an easy layup, but let him hook one off his left ear from 30 feet while falling down and it was apt as not to go in. Wier was as fantastic a guy with the basketball as these eyes have ever seen.

And there was Dick Ives, the kid from Diagonal, who had some sort of crazy jump shot in which he leaped in the air, seemed to throw both feet backward, and launched a shot which had no trajectory, but usually found its way into the basket. One night, more than 23 years ago, he threw in 19 baskets and five free throws against Chicago for a 43-point total which still stands as the Iowa single game record.

And everyone who was around here then will remember the Wilkinson boys from Utah. I don't even remember how they got to Iowa City, but I remember that Herb was about as smooth a guard as I've ever seen play. Shooting, rebounding, directing traffic, Herb richly deserved the all-Big Ten and All-America honors that came his way for three seasons. And Clayt, his big brother, wasn't far behind in ability or post-season honors.

And there was Ned Postels from Minnesota, the "upperclassman" as a junior on that 1945 championship team. And Jack Spencer, the famed "thin man" from Davenport who looked like a mild breeze might blow him over.

* * *

I REMEMBER A NIGHT IN MADISON — and I'm sure the Hawks who played then do, too—when a guy named Ed Mills shoved Spencer up into the fourth row of seats after Spencer reached to grab the ball from the Badgers' Bobby Cook in an out-of-bounds situation.

The defending champion Badgers won the game and Pops' Hawks vowed revenge when Wisconsin returned to Iowa City. They got it, too, and easily. That was the night the 5,000 students mobbed the place when the doors opened. Time and Life magazines both brought their cameras, but the action was mostly peaceful.

I remember, too, Bob Schulz squaring off in a pretty fair fight with some guy from Minnesota and everyone from both benches tried to join in. The band struck up The National Anthem, but the fighters were too busy to notice.

Those were exciting days, and wild nights, in Iowa basketball. Days of jubilation and nights of disappointment. Days of championship and near-championship. Nights of hysteria or heartbreak.

They'll replay a lot of those games this week as "Pops' boys" gather to see each other and talk with their old coach.

Could a man ask for better medicine?

This article written by Al Grady for the Iowa City Press Citizen was one I really enjoyed.

Murray Weir, and Bob Schulz, and the Star Spangled Banner.

He was only 5'8" tall, but Murray Weir played forward for the Hawks. He was very quick, and had an unorthodox style that made him difficult to guard. Murray led the country with a 21 point scoring average and was voted a first team All American.

There was a late season game against Minnesota in 1948 where the tensions were high between the teams. A fight broke out with seconds left in the game between Bob Schulz and Minnesota player Pete Tapsak. Schulz was a very tough and physical player for Iowa. Both benches cleared and numerous punches were thrown. To get the players to stop, the band started playing the Star Spangled Banner. Finally, between the officials and the band, order was restored and both Schulz and Tapsak were ejected. The game ended with Iowa winning 54-50.

It's the only time I ever remember the band playing a patriotic song to try to stop a fight!

Paul Brechler and Pops Harrison

In the spring of 1950 I was working at Bremers and answered the phone. It was the University of Iowa Athletic Director Paul Brechler. He wanted to talk to me about our basketball coach Pops Harrison. There was talk around town that he might be losing his job.

I was friends with several current and former basketball players and Mr. Brechler wanted to know if I was supporting him or Pops Harrison. I told him I was backing Pops Harrison.

Mr. Brechler told be two things about the coach's recent actions. First, he had been fixing grades for his players. Second, he had been selling tickets to the basketball games and pocketing the money.

I then told Mr. Brechler that if Pops Harrison was doing those things he should not be our coach. Later that month, Pops was fired by Paul Brechler.

A few years later Dave Danner and other former basketball players from the 1940's were together for a party and several them were wondering why their former coach was not retained by Iowa.

I told them my story and they were amazed. Danner, a very good friend of mine, said, "That explains who took my basketball tickets!" He asked me why I hadn't ever told him this before. I said, "Because you never asked me!"

Jack Spencer and Murray Wier are looking at the new university styled "SCOOP" hat by Resistol featured exclusively by BREMERS.

Jack has selected a tan herringbone Shetland topcoat while Murray is wearing a Bal model Donegal tweed topcoat... Both topcoats are tailored and styled by Mt. Rock... another exclusive brand at BREMERS.

Posed by:
Murray Wier
Jack Spencer
Salesman, "Murph" Murphey

"As Murph remembers…"
How We Met

Francis St. John was a good friend. He worked with me at Bremers when I was in my twenties and still a single young man. At one point Francis was in Mercy Hospital for a medical concern and I went to visit him. I noticed Louise Barnes, who was a nurse at Mercy Hospital in the hallway. She was one of Francis' nurses. When I came to visit she would bring him water, check his temperature and make sure he was feeling all right. Francis introduced us during one of my visits. I had noticed her downtown, but this was the first time we had spoken. Later after I had left his room, he found out that Louise wasn't dating anyone at the time and that she thought I was really handsome. So he suggested or 'put the bug in my ear' that I should ask her out. Several days later, Louise and I went on our first date to a City High football game. The dating turned into 65 years of marriage and seven children, ten grandchildren and three great grandchildren; not to mention many more football games.

"As Louise remembers…"
How We Met

I saw Murph one day walking in downtown Iowa City. He looked really handsome to me. I smiled and he smiled back, and I thought, wow! Several days later my cousin, Lois and I went into Bremers and he waited on us, but I thought he only seemed interested in Lois. Then, I saw him while I was working my shift as a nurse at Mercy Hospital. He was walking down the hall and I asked without thinking, "Why are you limping?" He explained that he had had polio as a child. I apologized.

A little while later, his good friend, Francis St. John was in the hospital, and Murph came to visit him. So, I decided maybe Francis needed some cold water, and delivered some to his room. While I was there, Francis introduced me to Murph. The next day, I made an excuse to go into Francis' room and he asked me if I was seeing anyone. He told me that Murph was interested in me. I was interested too. So, Francis said maybe he could help a bit, and put a "bug" in Murph's ear. It didn't take Murph too long to ask me out, and we went to a football game. Little did I know how many football games were in our future!

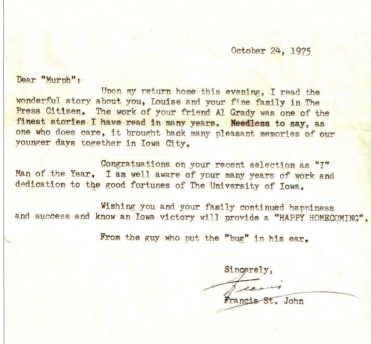

A Letter from Francis St. John

My Bremers life spanning 56 years

Bremers Men's Store was an important part of my life for 56 years. When I was a University of Iowa student, I used to ride the bus to the campus everyday. Harold Reedquist, the manager of Bremers Men's Store would often be on the bus with me. He noticed that I took my appearance very seriously, as I always made sure my shirt was pressed and my shoes were shined. In 1944, he offered me a summer job. The first month I worked really hard and led the staff in sales. I knew this was the career for me and abandoned my effort to earn a history degree at Iowa. I've never regretted that decision.

I had no idea how much work the job would be or how much fun I would have. I worked at Bremer's for five years before I met and married Louise Barnes of Washington, Iowa. We had seven children and they have all worked at the store in some capacity. Everyone helped deliver Bremers' calendars door to door in the summer. Jim, Joe and John all worked as salesmen. Ann and Mary Sue worked in the office. Jeff and Jerry helped make deliveries at Christmas time to customers awaiting tailored suits and beautifully wrapped gifts. If the store needed cleaning or I needed to go in after hours, I could always count on one of my children coming along to help or just to keep me company. They spent a lot of time with me in the basement, while I priced all of the clothing and checked in our entire inventory.

I look back at my years at Bremers... starting as a salesman, then being promoted the next year to hat buyer. I moved up the management ladder: assistant furnishings manager, assistant clothing manager and finally clothing buyer. I saw trends come and go... leisure suits, Nehru jackets, bell-bottom jeans and ties of all widths. We sold lots of Levis and lots of Iowa merchandise. We had our own tailor shop downstairs and could alter a suit or pair of pants to fit anyone perfectly.

On March 22, 1963 Bremers was destroyed in a fire. An arsonist who was actually trying to burn Lubins Drug Store, the store right next door, set it. I remember getting the phone call in the middle of the night that Bremers was on fire. It was gut wrenching. When I got downtown there was nothing left but the front of the building, it looked like a Hollywood movie set. As frustrating as the loss of Bremers was, our desire to stay in business was even stronger.

In the summer of 1963, Lloyd Berger and I bought Bremers. We were excited about making Bremers our own and continuing its great tradition of serving our customers. Because we had developed friendships with our customers, they followed us to our 'temporary store'. I had the philosophy that when *you shopped at Bremers you didn't just get what we had; you got what you wanted.* We could always order the right size or the right color. We started operating out of a

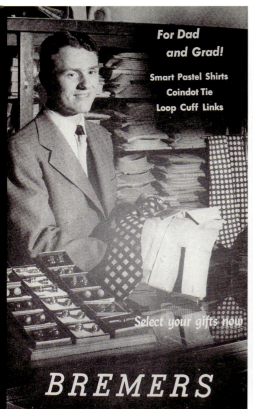

I am selling a football player a necktie.

Murph in his office at Bremers while being interviewed about the Hawkeyes by a reporter from the Minneapolis Tribune.

A Poem by Bev Buchanan in 1963

Down through the years there's always been
A store that men could learn on—
A landmark of good clothing taste
A gentleman could preen on.
A name that has withstood the test
Of time and Great Depression
Of wars, of floods, inflation.
Competition and recession.
And so it was a fearful shock
That sent our hopes all dwindling
To have some boorish villain
Turn our Bremers into kindling!
But fresh red blood began to flow
Through all discerning veins
On hearing news that Lloyd and Murph
Were taking up the reins.
No measly blaze could even phase
This mighty institution—
The soot and ash were merely part
Of her new evolution!
We raise our homburgs to her name—
We have no fears or tremors,
For all of Iowa City knows—
There'll always be a Bremers!

building on the corner of Washington and Dubuque Streets, where the Blackhawk Minipark is today. Our business was going well; the new store was under construction. We were going to make it work!

By mid-summer Bremers had reopened in its original location. The new store, back home at 120 East Washington Street, was beautiful. Lloyd and I had ordered red carpet; it was so warm and welcoming. The shelving and furnishing were walnut. All of the merchandise was top quality and well displayed. It was set up so well. Customers and sales staff alike really enjoyed being in the store. The office area upstairs had a big table where we would look at clothing samples that vendors brought us, where our staff would take breaks and where people would come in and talk. The "people who came in to talk" was probably one of the best parts of the job. Over the years there have been athletes, coaches, athletic directors, I-Club members, Iowa sports fans, university presidents and friends from across the country. It was fun to return home at the end of the day and let Louise know who had come into the store that day.

Bremers also made it a practice to hire university students. I have watched our salesmen become oil company executives, attorneys, and successful businessmen. My nephew Mike Kinney started in the clothing business at Bremers. He recently retired from Ralph Lauren where he was celebrated as their, Man of the Year and Designer of the Year.

Lloyd Berger was my business partner for 11 years. He died on December 31, 1974, after a short illness. He was only 48 years old. He had bought a pair of Bostonian boots and commented that they hurt his feet. He got a blister and it got infected. He went to the doctor and discovered he had cancer. It was so sudden and so unexpected! It had already gone throughout his body. He didn't want any visitors at the hospital. We wanted to help; we just didn't know how to help. It was very stressful for everyone. It was really a shock. Lloyd and I had worked well together and we had really expanded Bremers. We had two Bremers stores in Cedar Rapids, a Bremers and a Zipper in downtown in Iowa City and a Bremers and a Zipper in Iowa City's Sycamore Mall. I had another partner until 1984, my son John returned from working for Hart Schaffner & Marx clothing in Chicago to help run the company.

John and I sold Bremers in 2000. It was difficult to stop being in the retail business. Dillards came to the Coral Ridge Mall and carried many of the same clothing lines we did and were able to undercut our costs. Outlet stores were also changing people's buying habits. And, the move to casual dress in the business sector has altered the type of clothing people needed to buy. So, after fifty-six years of going downtown everyday… Bremers was over for me. The new owners closed the store a few years later.

I really feel that Bremers was an Iowa institution. We had lawyers, doctors, engineers, and other professional people graduate from Iowa and return to campus. They would always return to Bremers to visit and to buy clothing.

Earle and Louise standing proudly in Bremers

Murph, Moe Whitebook, Lloyd Berger, Francis St. John

John and Murph

JOHN HAYEK
HAYEK, BROWN, MORELAND & SMITH, L.L.P.
ATTORNEYS AT LAW

April 9, 2012

Mr. Earle Murphy
1692 Ridge Road
Iowa City, Iowa 52245

Dear Murph:

    I have often thought of you when I drive over the nicely paved alley behind our offices. I think the alley should be named the "Murphy Memorial Alley" in honor of your efforts many years ago to get it paved.

    I hope you and Louise are doing well. Pat and I think of you both fondly.

Very truly yours,

John Hayek

Bremers employees celebrating St. Patrick's Day in their green tuxedos.
For years, we hosted a luncheon for about 250 customers and friends.
We served corned beef and cabbage, green beer, and sang Irish songs.

Colonel Milton I. Bremer, AUS-Ret.
4922 Fulton Avenue
Sherman Oaks, California 91423-2005

February 17, 2000

Mr. Earle Murphy
1692 Ridge Road
Iowa City, Iowa 52245

Dear Earle:

By now, I hope you are able to kick back and say, I've had my fun and my problems, now the fun is mine and the problems are someone else's. You had a long run in business, and you are to be congratulated on that. I hope the years ahead give you good health and the opportunity to do all the things you wish.

My thanks also to you and John for your stewardship of the Bremer name. You maintained high standards of quality, and, obviously from the quotes of customers in the newspaper, equally high standards of service.

Should you find yourself escaping the cold and enjoying the sunshine of southern California, I hope you will take a minute to call and say hello. My best to you and your family.

Sincerely,

Milton Bremer wrote me a letter after the sale of Bremers. He lived within walking distance of my friends Chuck and Patricia Frandson in Sherman Oaks, California. So, one day while I was in California visiting the Frandson's I walked over to his house for a visit. It was nice to spend time with him and talk about Bremers.

"You're fortunate. Not everyone can wear camel hair."

The calendar had all of the schedules of Iowa sporting events. It also had the listings for the sororities and fraternities. When the shipment of calendars arrived, we would roll each one up and secure it with a rubber band; I'd put a wagon in the car, load up my family and head off to a neighborhood. I'd pull the wagon full of calendars, and the kids would quickly deliver them door-to-door. Everyone loved getting their calendar, and it was great advertising!

THE UNIVERSITY OF IOWA

April 20, 1999

Mr. Earl Murphy
Bremers
120 E. Washington Street
Iowa City, IA 52240

Dear Earl:

Your town and your university are indebted to you for 53 years of outstanding service as friend to all through Bremers and through your many varied civic activities. Like Old Capitol, you are a great Iowa institution. Congratulations and many thanks for all you do for all of us.

Sincerely yours,

Willard L. Boyd
Professor of Law and
President Emeritus
University of Iowa

I'm really proud of this letter from Willard Boyd. It is really something to have my life's work at Bremers compared to the Old Capitol.

Harry Bremer and his Lion

Harry Bremer went on an African Safari. He returned to Iowa City with two live lions. He kept them at his home, until he decided to donate them to the zoo at City Park. After the lions died Harry sent one to a taxidermist. One day he brought the lion to Bremers so he could pose for his Christmas card picture. Harry sure had some interesting ideas.

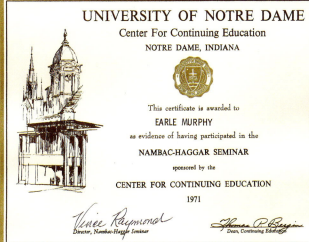

My introduction to computers

In 1971, I attended a four-day seminar given by Haggar Clothing Company. Vince Raymond was the instructor. I was really interested in everything they had to say. There was great information that I knew I could use at Bremers. Everyone had a computer on his desk. I even had my own computer for the training. Computers were new, and really new to me. Computers were the thing; they were something everyone was going to be using! Going to South Bend for the continuing education class was great. I got a lot out of it.

Bremers street view photo, circa 1950

Bremers sold Iowa apparel in the "Hawk Shop"

We were one of the first stores to sell Hawkeye merchandise. These photos were taken in the mid 1970's and used in our Bremers "Hawk Shop" brochure.

My son, Jerry Murphy receives the football. He's wearing his Iowa shirt, which was sold at Bremers.

Jim Blank, Rhea Folkers, John McKenna

John McKenna, Rhea Folkers

Jim Blank models an Iowa football jersey, and a Hawkeye sport coat and tie.

My Bremers Family

I was fortunate to have several great employees while I owned Bremers. Of course, my business partners Lloyd Berger and John Murphy were instrumental to our success. John McKenna and Nyle Kruse both did a great job and had long careers with Bremers. Other managers and salesmen I'd like to acknowledge include Ed Jones, Joe Messenger, Jim Blank, Mark Walz, Bob McCool, David Ferris, Jim Murphy, Joe Murphy, and Bill Witt. I am very thankful to all of them and everyone else who worked at Bremers.

Three employees who worked for us were John Buchanan, John Falb, and my nephew Mike Kinney. Each of them had successful business careers and they have made generous financial contributions to the University of Iowa. That makes me proud.

John McKenna walking up to the Bremers office

BREMERS
120 E. Washington St.
Downtown Iowa City

Lloyd Berger at our Zipper clothing store in Sycamore Mall

販売への結集

ノー セール　ノー ジョブ
No Sale. No Job

I was in Osaka, Japan in 1972, visiting the Mancillas suit company. As I was walking through the factory, I commented how much I liked the sign that was on the wall. Right away, they took it off the wall and gave it to me. It's not positive… but it's true!

> If you think you are beaten, you are:
> If you think you dare not, you don't
> If you'd like to win, but think you can't,
> It's almost a cinch you won't.
> If you think you'll lose, you're lost,
> For out in the world we find
> Success begins with a fellow's will:
> It's all in the state of mind.
> Life's battles don't always go
> To the stronger or faster man;
> But soon or late the man who wins
> Is the one who thinks he can.

This poster was upstairs in the office at Bremers. I thought that if you didn't believe you could make a sale…you probably wouldn't get it done. And making sales was very important for our business and made an impact on our salesmen's commission.

Dick Woodard and Dr. Ralph Woodard

Dick and Ralph Woodard are brothers from Fort Dodge, Iowa. Dick Woodard played center and linebacker for Iowa and was drafted by the New York Giants in 1948. He played in the NFL with Frank Gifford, Emlen Tunnell, Sammy Baugh, and Tom Landry during his five year professional career. He injured his knee in 1954, retired from football, and moved to the Quad Cities.

Dick is an extremely loyal and involved Hawkeye fan. For years, he would attend every Johnson County I-Club breakfast, waking up around 4 a.m. to drive over from the Quad Cities.

Dr. Ralph Woodard was a four year starter at Iowa, playing in his first Big Ten game at the young age of 17. In a game against Indiana his senior year, he was clipped going downfield to cover a punt return. He sustained a compound fracture leg injury, ending his football career.

Ralph was an excellent student and received the prestigious Nile Kinnick Scholarship while at Iowa. He received his medical degree in 1954, and practiced general surgery in Fort Dodge for 36 years.

Ralph and his wonderful wife, Martha, met in high school. Her maiden name was Pray. Her father had a plumbing business. His trucks had signs that said, "Pray for Better Plumbing." Louise and I always enjoyed visiting with Ralph and Martha when they came to Iowa City on football weekends.

Ralph passed away in 2014, but not before enjoying the athletic success of his grandson, Kirk Cousins. Kirk was a star quarterback at Michigan State, and currently plays for the Washington Redskins.

Bill Kay, Ralph & Dick Woodard, Ray Carlson and Murph

Herb and Scott Thompson
Father and Son Iowa Basketball Most Valuable Players

Herb Thompson came to the University of Iowa from Forest City, where he was a First-Team All-State basketball player in 1949. Herb was a good scorer who could really jump. He was named the Most Valuable Player for the Hawkeyes after the 1953 season. Herb became a teacher and successful basketball coach at Moline High School.

Scott Thompson was an All-State player for Moline High School in 1972, where he was coached by his father. Scott also starred at Iowa, and amazingly in 1976, like his father, was named the Most Valuable Player.

What a great achievement for a father and son.

Herb and I became good friends. During a recent phone call he joked that I had ruined his wedding night. Herb had purchased a new pair of pajamas from Bremers for his honeymoon. He wanted them mailed to him in a few days. I decided to pull a prank on him, and did not put the full pajama set in the gift box.

The first night he opened the box and there was a nicely folded top, but no pajama bottom. We got him pretty good...and I gave him the bottoms when he returned from his honeymoon. Herb still reminds me of it over sixty years later.

Oh well, I'm sure everything worked out just fine that evening.

Gimpy

I went down the street to meet with my attorney, Bill Meardon. On the way in his receptionist called me *Gimpy*. Bill overheard what she said and explained she shouldn't call me that. Yes, I walked with a limp, but he felt talking to me that way was impolite. So, after our meeting and on the way out she calls me Gimpy again, even after Bill told her not to. He later married her. I knew that she was just having fun with me.

"Murph remembers..."

The Evashevski Era Coaches

Bump Elliott told me that one day all of the coaches went for a ride before practice. Whitey Piro, Robert Flora, Forest Evashevski, Bump Elliott all relaxed and fell asleep. To make it worse the driver, Archie Kodros, got lost. When the coaches woke up, they realized they were going to be about 15 minutes late for practice. Bump said it was the funniest thing for all of the coaches to walk onto the practice field late, when all of the players were already there. At that time Iowa was known as the State University of Iowa as the S.U.I. sweatshirts show.

L-R: Whitey Piro, Bob Flora, Forest Evashevski, Bump Elliott, and Archie Kodros

Jeff Langston, Don Norton, and Coach Forest Evashevski

Jim Milani and Evy

Jim Milani was an excellent running back for Iowa in 1952, Evy's first year coaching. He was also an excellent student, and received a $500 Nile Kinnick Scholarship.

Evy would call Jim a "poor man's Dusty Rice", which upset him very much. Jim asked Evy to stop saying it. George "Dusty" Rice was also on the team and a talented defensive back and running back.

To maintain the upper hand, Evy called him the name one more time, and Jim Milani walked off the practice field and quit the team.

The next day Evy called me at work and asked me to help get Jim back on the team. I told him that I would not get involved as Jim was his own man, very intelligent, and able to make his own decisions. Evy quickly hung up on me.

Jim never returned to the team and instead concentrated on academics. He graduated from Iowa Law School and practices in Centerville, Iowa.

Jim Milani and his custom made suit

Jim ordered a custom made Hart Schaffner & Marx suit. I helped fit him and sent in the order. He returned to Bremers when it arrived.

When he tried on the coat the sleeves were way too long, covering his fingers. I was terrified that I had screwed up and I went to get a tailor.

The tailor looked at the coat and said the sleeve length looked okay to him.

Jim really tricked me and he busted out laughing. He was able to throw his back out, making the sleeves appear to be way too long.

Jim really got me good. I was relieved that the suit fit okay. I still laugh about it to this day!

The "Fainting Irish" football game in 1953

Iowa's football game at Notre Dame in 1953 was one of my most memorable.

Notre Dame was 8–0 and ranked #1 in the country. Forest Evashevski was our coach and we had a 7-0 lead late in the second quarter. Notre Dame had the ball on Iowa's 12 yard line with seconds left and no timeouts remaining. A Notre Dame lineman faked an injury to stop the clock. They scored on their next play, the final play of the half, to tie the score at 7-7.

Iowa led Notre Dame 14 – 7 in the closing seconds of the fourth quarter. Notre Dame was driving for a score and again, they were out of timeouts. It was Coach Frank Leahy's game plan that when they were out of timeouts to fake an injury to stop the clock. This time it was the right tackles job to "suffer" an injury. So with six seconds left in the game, their right tackle was down on the ground screaming in pain and the clock was stopped again. Notre Dame scored with a pass play and made the extra point and the game ended in a 14-14 tie.

Notre Dame Heisman trophy winner Johnny Lattner played in the game and joked, "I thought Forest Evashevski was going to come across the field and kill Leahy."

Notre Dame was widely criticized by the media and its own fan base and labeled as the Fainting Irish.

I love the quote made by Forest Evashevski the following week. He parodied the famous sportswriter Grantland Rice at an Iowa pep rally, saying, *"When the one great scorer comes to write against your name, he writes not whether you won or lost, but how come we got gypped at Notre Dame."*

This game made me, a proud Irish Catholic, always root a little harder against Notre Dame.

Decade Four | 1953-1962 | 49

Photo of Kinnick Stadium and surrounding area, 1956

Jim Gibbons touchdown reception to defeat Ohio State, November 17, 1956. This catch sent us to the Rose Bowl!
note the football in the top right corner

Randy Duncan
Iowa Football

Randy was a great quarterback for Iowa. As Iowa's #25, he was the runner up for the Heisman Award. During the 1958 football season he led the Hawkeyes to the Rose Bowl. He won many awards: All American, the Grantland Rice Award, All Big Ten first team, Most Valuable Player, United Press and Sportswriters MVP, and the Walter Camp trophy as Helms Foundation's Player of the Year.

He posed in the Cedar Rapids airport before he traveled to the Rose Bowl game. While he was in Pasadena he met Jane Mansfield who was the sexist actress at the time. He had said before the trip to California that he wanted to meet her. And after Iowa won the game, he did better than that... he got to give her a kiss.

He lived above the Varsity Theatre with Arnie Davidson and Bert Belt. He was a smart player and knew a lot of trick plays. At one home game I watched one of those plays unfold. Iowa was in formation to receive a punt from the opposing team. The Iowa punt returner was Don Debrino. After he caught the ball, he raised the football near his head. I yelled to Louise, "Watch this, he's gonna give it to Smith." We watched him hand the football to Smith, who ran about 40 yards for a touchdown. Louise was impressed that I had guessed what was going to happen, but Randy had told me to look out for this very play!

He returned to Iowa City in 2006 for the celebration of the 1956 and 1958 Rose Bowl victories. The Garden Club luncheon included the presentation of the Grantland Rice trophy, which the 1958 team won for being named National Champions. Randy was able to spend time with some of his former coaches and teammates.

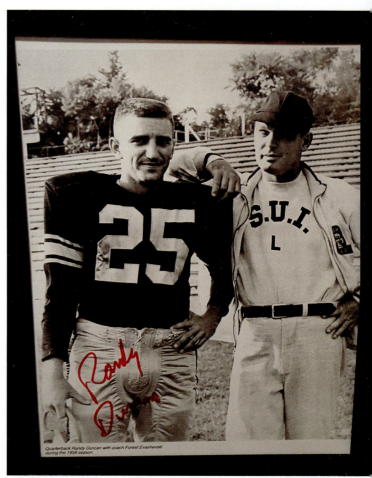

Photo Courtesy of Mark Wilson

Decade Four | 1953-1962 — 51

Willie Fleming makes another nice run during the 1958 season.
I love this picture and had it framed and on the back wall of Bremers for years.
The picture is now displayed inside of Murphy's Bar & Grill in Riverside, Iowa.

The Grantland Rice Trophy National Championship Team of 1958

Forest Evashevski
The coach and the athletic director

Forest Evashevski was a great football coach at Iowa for nine years, from 1952-60. He led Iowa to Rose Bowl victories in 1957 and 1959. He resigned to become Athletic Director in 1960. Many thought if he would have continued in coaching, he would have built a football dynasty at Iowa.

Jerry Burns, who replaced him as Iowa's football coach, made these comments about Evy in 1992. "I had the honor to work with coaching greats like Vince Lombardi and Bud Grant, both of whom coached in Super Bowls, but I'm not sure that the best of them all wasn't Forest Evashevski. Evy was a genius on the football field. And of all the teams I ever worked with – and this included Super Bowl teams at Minnesota and Green Bay – I really feel the greatest at its level of competition was the 1958 Iowa team. I have never seen a better running back than Willie Fleming – and Randy Duncan has to rank with the best of all quarterbacks."

That's very high praise and speaks volumes about the coaching ability of Evy.

Evy was intelligent, charismatic, powerful, feared, and controlling. Those attributes worked well for being a great football coach, but did not transfer as well to being a good athletic director. Evy had well known feuds with his predecessor, Athletic Director Paul Brechler, as well as Burns' head coaching successor, Ray Nagel. I also had my own feuds with Evy. Once, in the mid 1960's, Evy and I had major disagreements over how he was treating football coach Jerry Burns. The next week, Ruth Evashevski came into the store and said, "I can't shop here anymore." Bremers was now "off-limits" for the Evashevski family. She was sad because we had become good friends.

At the end of the 1969 season, things got wild around Iowa City regarding Evy and Ray Nagel. There was a player revolt against Ray Nagel, and suggestions circulating that Evy wanted to coach football again. Iowa quarterback Larry Lawrence came into Bremers during that time and asked me to take a ride in his car. We started circling the block and he asked me whose side I was on. Did I want Nagel fired? I told him no, I'm supporting Nagel, not Evy. With that, the car ride was over and I returned to work.

Numerous sportswriters and businessman stopped into Bremers during those weeks as the rumors were swirling. In January 1970, an assistant coach was dismissed for "disloyalty" to the program for supporting Evy. In February, Larry Lawrence and Tom Smith quit the team and transferred to the University of Miami. In May, the State Auditor of Iowa announced that the athletic department was under investigation for "padded expense" accounts.

After an investigation, the Iowa Board in Control of Athletics fired Ray Nagel and announced Forest Evashevski was resigning. After the announcement, support was strong for Nagel, and he was re-hired to coach the last year of his contract.

After nine great years as our football coach, and ten volatile years as our athletic director, the Evashevski Era at Iowa was over.

Photos Courtesy of Special Collections, University of Iowa Libraries

Joe Murphy and Hawkeye Players

JOEY MEETS THE BIG HAWKS—Joe Murphy, 15-month-old son of the Earl Murphys of Iowa City, got a close look at the two big seniors who hold Iowa's hopes at tackles this season. Shown as the Hawks opened practice Monday, they are John Burroughs (left), 220-pounder from Washington, D.C., and Mac Lewis, 289-pounder from Chicago.

In 1958, my son, Joe is pictured with two Iowa football players at the first practice of the season. Player #72 is John Burroughs and player #55 is Mac Lewis. Years later, John and Joe and Mac reunited at the 50th reunion of Iowa's winning Rose Bowl team.

Simon Estes

He was a good hurdler from Centerville, Iowa. He came to Iowa when Francis Cretzmeyer was the track coach. Simon only ran track for one year because he became committed to training his voice. He could really sing. While he was in college, one of his jobs was washing dishes at the back of Lubins Drugstore, next door to Bremers.

Years later, Lubins had been long gone and Bremers made it into an upbeat store called the Zipper. Simon was back in town for the rededication of the Old Capitol, and to perform. He came into Bremers to say hello. We walked into the Zipper and he showed me where he would have stood to wash dishes during his college days. He pretended to wash dishes and seemed to be reliving those times. His manager interrupted him and told him that it was time to go to the Old Capital event.

So, we walked over together. There were lots of people there to listen to him sing. Louise and the kids were already at the Old Capital sitting on blankets to watch his performance and I joined them.

Another time Simon was in town to give a concert at Hancher Auditorium and I knew he was staying at the Downtown Holiday Inn. We had just started having our Garden Club meeting at the hotel restaurant. I called Simon and invited him to join us for lunch. He said he had to rest his voice and wouldn't be able to come down. But, when I told him that his old coach Cretz was there, he said, "I'll be right down." I gave him a beautiful Iowa sweater at the luncheon. Later that night, at the concert at Hancher, when he came out for his first encore, he had replaced the top of his tux with that sweater, and the crowd loved it.

Bucky O'Connor

In April of 1958, Bucky O'Connor came into Bremers to see me. Bucky was the Iowa men's basketball coach and his teams were very successful during his eight years at the helm. In the 1955-1956 season they won 17 games in a row and played in the national championship game. This team was nicknamed the "Fabulous Five".

He was at the store because he wanted to get a nice new raincoat since he was heading to New York City to accept an award for his coaching success. We had just received a shipment of beautiful coats from Barracuda. I found a tan raglan sleeve style in just his size. It was just perfect! So he bought it and took it to New York City.

The Day of All Days

Several days after his trip to New York City, I was surprised to see him back in the store. Bucky comes over to me with the raincoat under his arm. He needs help because someone spilled coffee all over his new coat. I told him that Dave Todd at Paris Cleaners would get all the coffee stain out and not to worry! As he turned to leave, I asked him, "What's going to happen today?" He told me he was headed for La Porte City, near Waterloo, to attend a dinner in his honor.

Later that day, I found out that on his drive to La Porte City, he swerved to avoid a mother duck and her five ducklings as they were crossing the highway. He didn't notice the approaching traffic on highway 218. He hit a semi head-on. He was only 44 years old when he died in the accident.

Elwin Jolliffe, the treasurer at the U of I, and close friend of Bucky's, picked up the raincoat in the days after the tragic accident.

I think I was one of the last people to be with him that day.

Don Norton

Don Norton was a Hawkeye offensive end. He was a first team All American and MVP of the team in 1959. Coach Evashevski called him the best end he ever coached.

He was inducted into the UI Athletics Hall of Fame in 2015.

He was at Bremers and we were visiting in the upstairs office. When he left, he had both hands in his pockets and he managed to fall down the steps outside the office. He landed face down and split his pants. We were both laughing and discovered that he was going to need a new pair of pants. I made sure he was fixed up, compliments of Bremers.

Bob Jeter, the Day after Winning the 1959 Rose Bowl

I made arrangements with Bob Jeter, Willie Fleming, and John Burroughs that after they flew in to the Cedar Rapids airport, I'd be there to pick them up. I drove my new 1957 Oldsmobile. John had been one of the star players and he just wanted to go home and study.

Willie had scored two touchdowns and he needed to meet his buddies downtown and celebrate. Jeter had just played the game of his life, with 194 rushing yards in only nine carries. This included an 81-yard touchdown and earning the MVP of the game. Jeter said, "I'm going to Murphy's house. Our house was on Linn Street. He walked into the kitchen and spied what was left of our holiday turkey. Louise hadn't put it in the refrigerator yet. He asked, "Is that a turkey? Has it been deboned? Can I?" So, Ann, Jim, Louise and I watched him do it. He just relaxed and took care of that turkey, eating and talking. But, there was no discussion about the game; we just spent time together. There I was, with the MVP of the Rose Bowl in my kitchen…and we didn't talk sports at all!

John Burroughs ended up becoming ambassador to the African nations of Malawi and Uganda. Willie Fleming went on to have a long pro-career in Canada and is a member of the Canadian Football Hall of Fame. Bob Jeter played pro ball for the Green Bay Packers and the Chicago Bears.

The Spelling Bee

Gene Claussen and Herb Olsen started KXIC in 1960. We all enjoyed listening to Gene on the radio. Lloyd Berger always called him "Walter Cronkite", because he had an unusual, unforgettable and very recognizable voice. Dottie Ray was an interviewer on KXIC, and as part of her responsibilities, she hosted a spelling bee. I was asked to participate in one of their spelling bees with Dottie as the moderator. There were elementary school children on one team and adults on the other. Dottie looked at the first word and said, "Murph, we have a good one for you…" She handed the card with the word on it to a young girl on the other team to read. The girl smiled and asked me to spell clothes and I spelled it, c-l-o-t-h-s. All I remember hearing was Dottie's voice saying, "Incorrect."

So I was out and the girl was so excited she jumped for joy because she was still in the game. My family was at home listening on the radio, and they were mortified! I was teased for missing that word for a while. I may have been a great clothing salesman; I just misspelled one of the words of my trade.

Wilburn Hollis

Wilburn played football for Jerry Burns. In 1960, during his junior year, he became the starting quarterback. He led the Hawkeyes to a Big Ten Championship. He was one of the first black quarterbacks to earn All-American honors. The Sports Writers of America also featured him in Sporting News magazine for being selected as the quarterback for the scholastic All American football team. Wilburn started his senior year, leading the Hawkeyes to a 28-7 victory over California and the coveted #1 ranking. In just the second game of the season, the Iowa-USC game, he broke his right wrist. He was devastated because his season had ended much too soon.

Wilburn was not only hurting physically, but emotionally as well, because he knew he couldn't play football anymore. So he applied for an extension of eligibility from the Big Ten to see if he could sit out the rest of the season and play the next year. About a week later, he hears from Eric Wilson, the sports information representative for Iowa athletics. Eric tells Wilburn he HAS qualified for the extension. So, Wilburn comes into Bremers and tells me the good news. We hug, knowing good things will happen for him as a football player.

Two hours later he's back in the store. He looks sad. I ask him what's wrong. He tells me that unfortunately, Eric had misread the letter and he didn't make it. He won't play for Iowa again. He didn't get the eligibility waiver. And, oh boy, now he's so upset. He wanted to play football so badly. It is about 4:45, and I have fifteen minutes until closing the store. I had him sit and relax in the shoe department. Then I had him come home with me to the Linn Street house and we sat on the porch swing and talked.

I believe that since he had been an All American QB his junior year, he would have been one his senior year if he had been able to finish the season. We have continued our friendship. Wilburn now lives in Marion, Iowa and visited me a couple of years ago.

Jim Evashevski wrestling match upset

In 1962, Jim Evashevski was a very good wrestler for Iowa City High. I attended the district wrestling meet held at City High. We sat down next to Jim's mom, Ruth Evashevski.

In the district finals, Jim was going up against Mel Weiland from Cedar Rapids Jefferson. Mel was a senior and a two-time state champion. He had won 53 matches without a loss. Jim pinned Mel in 1 minute and 8 seconds! The crowd went wild.

In her excitement, Ruth gave me a kiss on the cheek. I said, "That kiss was for Evy right?" She said, "You bet it was!" That was one of the most exciting wrestling matches I've ever seen.....and the kiss wasn't bad either.

Coach Clyde Bean and Jim Evashevski

For 35 years, City High had only one head wrestling coach. From 1956-1991, Clyde Bean was a teacher and coach. He was also the head football coach from 1968-1980. Coach Bean was inducted into the Iowa Wrestling Hall of Fame in 1993.

We had a special Garden Club luncheon on homecoming weekend in the fall of 2006. It included players and coaches back for a reunion from the 1956, 1958 and 1991 Rose Bowl teams. Also attending were head coaches Forest Evashevski, Jerry Burns, Hayden Fry and Kirk Ferentz.

I asked Jim Evashevski to attend our Garden Club luncheon that day. As a surprise to Jim, I also called and invited his former coach Clyde Bean. I knew they had a special bond and would enjoy seeing each other. Jim was surprised and happy when he saw Clyde and they had a wonderful visit. It was a great reunion for all, and the Hawks beat Purdue the next day 47-17.

Murph Remembers...

Decade Five | 1963-1972

"Murph remembers…"

Dr. Jack Moyers, Earle Murphy, and getting the Amana V.I.P. open to the public

The first Amana Open golf tournament was held in Greenbrier, West Virginia, in 1967. The hosts decided that the event would be private and not open to the public. This would allow the golf pros and Amana participants to golf in privacy. The tournament was moved the following year to the University of Iowa's Finkbine golf course. As the date for the golf event approached, people in Iowa City were getting excited, including me.

Jack Moyers came into Bremers the week before the tournament to have a Pepsi with me. He said he had driven by Finkbine that morning and workers were busy putting a fence around the entire golf course. I asked him if he knew why they were doing that. He told me that the event was to be closed to the public and the fence would keep people out.

Well, I had been talking to my family about this golfing event; I had promised them they could come with me. We were looking forward to seeing Don Knotts and some other celebrities who were coming. I didn't want my wife and children to be disappointed; I was planning to take my sons to watch the pros play. The more I thought about it the madder I got. I told Jack Moyers that they just couldn't do that. The fence needed to come down. The event needed to be open to anyone who wanted to attend. I had to do something to fix it. As I started to leave the office Jack asked me where I was going. I said, "I'm going to get a lawyer and stop this." He told me there was no way I would be able to change it. He said there was no way I would win.

So I went to the law offices upstairs and talked with Bill Tucker. He listened to my complaint and said that interestingly enough the Iowa Law School had just had a mock trail on this very subject. Bill was just as set on getting the tournament open to the public as I was. I am not sure exactly what happened behind the scenes. I know Tucker spoke with the right people. I know that he explained the legalities of why it should not be closed to the public. I know I planned on attending the tournament on Monday morning… even if I had to cross the fence. I would go with my lawyer and my family at my side.

The day before the tournament, on Sunday afternoon at about four o'clock, I received a phone call from Jack Moyers. "Murph, you won!" He explained that the board had decided the Amana V.I.P. Golf tournament would be called the Amana V.I.P. Open. The public would be able to attend and admission would be $1.00 per person. The proceeds would go the Iowa Scholarship fund. I don't know exactly what was said at the meetings, I just know: I got it opened to the public. Later that evening, Louise and I quietly celebrated our victory with a glass of wine.

The Amana Open was played in Iowa City for 24 years. During that time it was a major fundraiser for Iowa athletic scholarships.

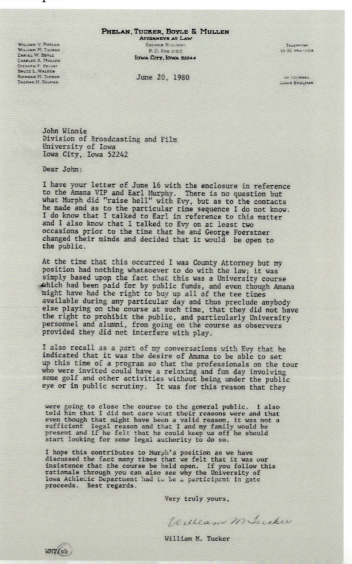

An opinion letter published in the Cedar Rapids Gazette in 1978 by Father Robert Welch

In its official program the 1978 Amana golf tournament on June 19 gave a historical look at the Amana VIPs written by Tait Cummins.

After relating that the first tournament was a closed affair just for pros and Amana people and held at Greenbrier in West Virginia in 1967, Cummins goes on to the stoy of the next year.

1968: Amana V.I.P. *'went public'* in 1968, thus adding an extra dimension that has pleased tens of thousands of Iowans and Midwesterners in the ensuing years, 1978 included. And, of course, Amana's V.I.P. placed a stalwart shoulder to the wheel in support of worthy causes."

The 1968 VIP, actually, added three new dimensions to the one of 1967.

#1 It was held at Iowa City Finkbine.
#2 It was thrown open to the public.
#3 It began the worthy contribution of proceeds to the Iowa athletic scholarship fund.

There is an interesting story about dimension #2 that has never been told publicly, but should have been. It is a stirring account of how one stubborn Irishman (enough for most causes) changed the character of the VIP or caused it to be changed.

Originally, when the VIP of '68 was set up by George Foerstner and Forest Evashevski, the latter who was then the Athletic Director at Iowa, it was not intended to be open to the public at all. Early in the week before the tournament a prominent member of the Iowa Athletic Board was having coffee with one Earl Murphy in the office of Bremers in Iowa City. Murph casually mentioned that it was great having the Amana in Iowa City so his sons could go out and watch some great pros play.

The quick answer of the *board man* was that the event was closed. There was no way any outsiders could get in. Foerstner had bought up all tee-times for the day. Evy, with his well-known personal proprietary attitude toward Finkbine, would assure a totally closed operation. The pros wanted to be left alone to relax, and the Amana personnel didn't want their amateur performances under public scrutiny.

All of this got Murph's Irish up and he informed the *board man* that Finkbine was public property, not private domain and if there was any question about it, he would be there on Monday morning with his sons and a lawyer!

The *board man* suggested Murph abandon such a losing cause and left the Bremers' office. Murph went up to the second floor of the Bremer building, presented the case to lawyer Bill Tucker. The latter got as steamed up as Murph, said he definitely has a case, and promised to be on hand early Monday morning.

Nothing happened that Murph was aware of the rest of the week; except for several reminders to Earl from the *board man* that there was simply no way Murph could win. Then, on Sunday afternoon at 4p.m., the day before the VIP, Murph got a call from the *board man* saying, "You win. The tournament is now open to the public. There will be a charge of $1.00 per person with the proceeds to be given to the Iowa Athletic department for scholarship help."

That is the story of how one man changed things just because he felt they should be changed, knew how to go about it, and had the guts to do something. It would be interesting to know the story of what went on behind the scenes when Foerstner and Evy were confronted with a new kind of Murphy's Law.

(Father Welch knew what was going on... we talked a lot!)

Murph Remembers...

Cap Logos

I believe that Amana was the first to put their corporate logo on golf pro apparel. In 1968, Julius Boros wore an Amana VIP cap in the PGA Championship. Dave Stockton, Miller Barber, Lou Graham, and several other golfers wore the caps and were paid $50.00 a week. Today, all golf professionals have numerous logos on their caps, shirts, and golf bags. And Amana started it all!

Jerry Burns   Iowa Football Coach

Jerry Burns coached under Forest Evashevski. He started with the Hawks in 1954 as the freshman coach. In 1955, he was the head backfield coach working with the defense and helping with recruiting. In 1961, when Evy decided to retire as head coach to become Iowa's Athletic Director, Evy appointed Jerry to succeed him as Iowa's head football coach. Jerry was only 34 years old at the time.

Jerry Burns and his wife, Marlyn, and Louise and I were good friends. We attended St. Mary's Church together. Our children were similar ages. We named our sixth child Jerry, after Jerry Burns. We were friends apart from Iowa athletics. We got along well. His career at Iowa was not as successful as his predecessor Evy's had been. So, after four years and a 16-27-2 record, Jerry was fired.

Who's calling first… Vince Lombardi or George Allen?
One Sunday, Louise and I were taking an afternoon drive and decided to drop in on Jerry and Marlyn. When we arrived he was glad to see us, but he told us he might have to stop chatting with us, because he was expecting an important phone call. He told us that we couldn't use the phone. He was hoping to receive a phone call from either Vince Lombardi or George Allen. Jerry told us he would say 'yes' to the first coach who called. While we were there, the phone rang and Jerry quickly went to his bedroom to take the call. Marlyn and Louise and I just sat quietly, waiting for whatever changes were coming to their lives. When Jerry came back to the living room he said, "I'm now a Packer!" We congratulated him and returned home so Marlyn and Jerry could discuss their future.

Going to a Packer Game
The next football season, Father Robert Welch made plans for a group of us to travel to watch a Chicago Bears – Green Bay Packers game on Sunday, September 24, 1967. Besides Father Welch, a teacher at the UI School of Religion, we had Dr. John McDonald and Red Hasting, a Chevrolet dealer in Sterling, Illinois. When we arrived at Lambeau Field, Jerry met us to give us our tickets. He handed them to the other three guys and told me that I was going to the press box with him. I was thrilled to death! About 15 minutes before kickoff we got in the booth, and Jerry introduced me to the other four coaches. They gave me a 'fish handshake' and I immediately realized that I wasn't wanted. I watched out the window of the press box before the game as Vince Lombardi, who was down on the field, gave the coaches a fist pump salute and the coaches in the booth enthusiastically returned the gesture.

After the band played the National Anthem I walked

My press box pass for the Packers game

out. I knew I needed to leave. I headed to the middle of stadium. I noticed a man was walking behind me, so I asked him if he was following me. He told me he worked for the Green Bay organization. Coach Burns had told him to take care of me and get me whatever I needed. I told him I was okay. I had noticed a nice recliner chair nearby, and I wanted to sit right there. I was up in the press box, in the middle of the stadium, on about the 40-yard line; it was a beautiful place to watch the game!

Down the aisle on my right, there were two English speaking French Canadian sports broadcasters who were covering the game in French for a radio station back in Quebec, Canada. The announcer was dressed in a very large overcoat, and had several scarves around his neck, to ward off the wind and the chilly 45-degree temperature. Their microphone was really large and had some type of soft gauze wrapped around it to mute the sound of the wind.

One broadcaster slowly approached me and asked if I knew anything about the teams or the game. I told him I knew Bob Jeter, the defensive halfback. I let him know that I didn't know everything, but I knew football. He would talk with me and then return to his broadcasting area and speak in French with his partner.

I talked with him a little bit and added some color commentary. He told me that CBS was televising the game and was coming to take some shots of them doing their broadcast. He wanted me to join them at their announcing table. So, I joined them and ended up sharing lots of information about the game and football players. I had a ball! A CBS cameraman did come and take a short clip of us covering the game, which was broadcast nationally.

After the game, Jerry found me with the French broadcasters and apologized to me. "Man, did you do the right thing," he said, referring to my decision to leave the coaches box. Then he said, "You were the first friend I invited into the coaches box, and you'll be the last."

After the game, we all returned to Iowa City. The next day, I was walking from Bremers down Washington Street to the bank and a woman walks up to me.
"Hey, are you Murph?"
"Yes, I am."
"Were you standing next to the guy that was talking French at the Packers game?"
"Yes, I was."
"Great, I just won $50 from my husband!"

Jerry was with the Packers for two years and they won the Super Bowl both of those years.

This was the Hawkeye logo when Jerry Burns coached at Iowa.

Paul Krause / NFL record 81 career interceptions

Paul Krause and I became good friends when he played football for the Hawkeyes in the early 1960's. I think he's one of the best all-around athletes to ever play at Iowa.

Paul earned all-state honors in football, basketball, baseball, and track. He grew up in Flint, Michigan, and was recruited to Iowa by Jerry Burns. Paul played safety, wide receiver, and returned kicks for the Hawkeyes. He had great speed and quickness, and good size at 6'3" 190 lbs.

Many thought he would play professional baseball. Paul was a great center fielder, a good hitter, and earned All-American honors his sophomore year at Iowa. He was drafted into the major leagues, but turned down the offer. His junior year he injured his shoulder playing football, limiting his chances for a pro baseball career.

Paul was drafted in the second round of the 1964 NFL draft by the Washington Redskins. As a rookie, he led the league in interceptions. After four seasons and 28 interceptions with the Redskins, he was traded to the Minnesota Vikings. With the Vikings, he played in four Super Bowls and was an eight time Pro Bowl selection.

Paul Krause currently holds the all-time NFL record with 81 interceptions. It's a record that may never be broken. He was often referred to as the Vikings "Center Fielder" due to history as a baseball player, and success at catching interceptions. He also recovered 19 fumbles, returning them for 163 yards and three touchdowns. During his 16 years playing professional football, Paul only missed two games due to injury.

Paul was elected into the Pro Football Hall of Fame in 1998. Jerry Burns, who also coached for the Vikings during Paul's career, introduced him at his Hall of Fame ceremony.

Paul Krause, Wally Hilgenberg, Mike Reilly, and all Iowa seniors had their final home game cancelled because of the assassination of President Kennedy

Lloyd Berger and the Vietnam Protest

Lloyd Berger was the co-owner of Bremers and a fantastic businessman. In the spring of 1970, the Vietnam protests were going strong and downtown establishments were getting their windows broken by college students using rocks and crowbars.

One day, we heard a rumor that Bremers was going to be targeted that evening. Lloyd was furious and he was not going to sit still while the protesters broke our windows and possibly looted our store.

Lloyd had served in France and Germany in World War II. He decided that evening he was going to bring one of his guns to the store and he told me, "I'm going to kill the first son of a bitch that comes into the store."

I said, "My God, what are you doing Lloyd?" I asked him not to do it and started to walk away. He said, "Where are you going?" I said, "I'm going home and you should too."

Later that evening, a protester broke a window with a crowbar, and started walking into the store. Lloyd was in the middle of the store and started approaching the man with his gun.

Thankfully, a policeman tackled him before Lloyd could shoot him!

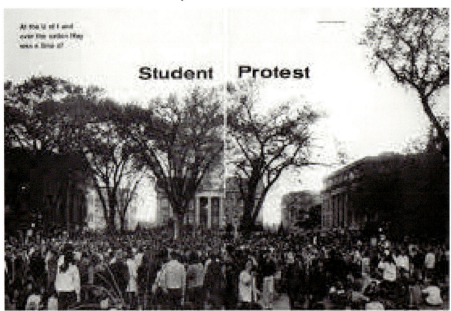

Hong Kong, China 1972 for the Ready to Wear Festival

Flying into Hong Kong we saw colors everywhere. They were blue and white and green and red, and we found out it was their laundry hanging to dry on the top of their apartments. It looked like flags flying and was really beautiful.

We stayed at the luxurious Hong Kong Hilton. The culture and the people were fun for Louise because just about everyone was her size. I remember her saying, "I'm just like everybody here." It was very British since it hadn't been turned over to the Chinese government yet. We ordered tea and were surprised to get plain old Lipton tea... we were expecting something fancy.

We took a ferry from Hong Kong to Macau, and then traveled to Tokyo, Japan. We were selling clothing at Bremers that was being manufactured in Tokyo. The brand was Mancillas International. The vendor was actually from Mexico, but he was working in Japan because that was where his garment factories were located. We went to Japan to tour the facilities. All of the Japanese women were sewing with their Singer sewing machines. Louise thought it was fascinating that they used the same brand of sewing machine she had back in Iowa. The workers were housed and fed on site. The women were proud to be part of the company. Kabuki type music was playing in the background. It was interesting to watch how the clothing was assembled.

While I went to meetings Louise stayed and did interesting things around the hotel. When we shopped I was used to just paying the price marked on the item; instead we had to barter. I wasn't very good at it and I bet I over paid!

Louise and I loved this trip, and it was a wonderful experience.

Governor Robert Ray and Louise on TV.

The year was 1972, and Louise and I went to the Fieldhouse to see a basketball game. Once we arrived we were invited to sit courtside. And we just happen to sit next to Iowa's Governor, Bob Ray. His highway patrolman was sitting right behind him. The governor started visiting with Louise and he also shared his popcorn with her. She was really dressed in style and was wearing beautiful boots she had bought in Japan. She looked like a million bucks. The TV camera went on, and our nephew watching in Omaha, Nebraska later said, "What was Aunt Louise doing with the governor, chatting and eating popcorn?"

So, Herky notices that the governor is at the game and he comes over and pays attention to him. He also wanted Louise to dance with him, which she did enthusiastically. I think the cameraman and Herky the Hawk both thought Louise was the governor's wife.

Murphy Family Photo - 1969 *Top row:* Earle, Ann, and Jim
Middle row: Family dog Taffy, Jeff, John, Louise, Mary Sue, and Jerry   *Bottom row:* Joe

Murph Remembers...

Francis X Cretzmeyer
Iowa Track Coach

Francis X Cretzmeyer was a fantastic track athlete and coach for the University of Iowa. He was a great person and friend. As an athlete, his times in the 220-meter hurdles were some of the best in the world. "Cretz" also excelled in the long jump, high jump, and javelin. He was known as "the runner with glasses." He was a contemporary of Jesse Owens, and competed in numerous events against the legendary athlete, often finishing in second place. In 1936, he was awarded the Big Ten Medal of Honor for his combined achievements in athletics and academics.

"Cretz" coached track and cross country at Iowa from 1948-1978 and led the Hawkeyes to five Big Ten team titles. He was one of the first coaches to recruit African-American athletes to run long distances. One of the first and best was Charles (Deacon) Jones. As a sophomore in 1955, Deacon Jones became the first African-American NCAA cross country champion. In 1957, he added an NCAA title in the two-mile run. During track meets held in southern states, often times hotel rooms, bathrooms, restaurants, and water fountains were "for whites only." On one trip, since Deacon Jones wasn't allowed to stay in the hotel because of his skin color, his white head coach "Cretz" and white teammates spent the nights with him in a train boxcar.

Ted Wheeler was another African-American trailblazer for Iowa as a track athlete and coach. Ted was a four-time Big Ten Champion in the 880 yard and mile run in the 1956 Big Ten indoor and outdoor meets. In 1978, Ted Wheeler was named the first African-America head coach at the University of Iowa.

Larry Wieczorek was a six-time Big Ten Champion in cross country and track for Iowa in the late 1960's. He was another protégé of "Cretz" that followed him into the coaching profession at Iowa. I was really happy for him when his Hawkeye team won the 2011 Big Ten Outdoor Championship, held on our home track. Larry was also named the 2011 Big Ten Coach of the Year.

The Olympic-sized track at the University of Iowa, completed in 1986, is named the Francis X Cretzmeyer Track. In the 1970's and 1980's, I would often see "Cretz" at the local Pumpernickel Restaurant. He was a good friend of the owner Ron Ameche. The Pumpernickel was a very popular place for coaches, businessmen, and University of Iowa employees.

Francis X Cretzmeyer died on April 2, 2001. On April 13, I hosted a Garden Club luncheon for his friends and family to commemorate his wonderful life. Before the event, I received a heartfelt note of admiration about "Cretz" from Dr. Robert Soper.

April 4 2001
723 Bayard St.
Iowa City, IA

Dear Murph—

I understand that our Garden Club is going to meet April 13th to commemorate the loss of one of our most beloved senior members, Francis X. Cretzmeyer. Regrettably, Helene and I will be driving to Ohio that day to officially welcome our 13th grandchild, a boy, into our family. Perhaps this is symbolic of the Easter message of resurrection, which no doubt Cretz is now enjoying.

You may not recall that Cretz and I both were born and raised in Emmetsburg, Iowa. Our parents were great friends, but since I am 13 years his junior, our paths did not really cross until I began Medical School here in 1947. Since then, our boys have been friends with the two younger Cretzmeyers, and I have basked in the reflected glory of my Emmetsburg compatriot's outstanding achievements in Track and Field at the University. But I do recall vividly what an icon he was during his Emmetsburg High School sports career, a feat which he continued in college and during his wonderfully long and outstanding tenure as Track Coach at the University of Iowa. Real sports giants are few and far between, but Francis X. Cretzmeyer joins Nile Kinnick and a handful of others to have earned that accolade. He will be sorely missed..

Bob
Bob and Helene Soper

HONORING
OWA'S CRETZMEYER
in his 25th year

FRANCIS X. CRETZMEYER
University of Iowa

SATURDAY EVENING — DECEMBER 2, 1972

CAROUSEL
IOWA CITY, IOWA

"THE COACH"

A coach usually has a very special quality in him. It's a quality that makes young people feel needed and useful. This applies to the gifted athlete, the average athlete and the below average athlete. Everybody needs someone to help them feel secure upon leaving their high school days and entering the computerized college life. So many times the new collegiate feels the institution to be extremely impersonal. And more times than not, he's right. Our coach, like many other coaches, is a person boys can talk to. He has the know how in making them feel they can and do belong. Our coach recognized that each person is in his own way a special human being with different desires and goals. And it takes a special person to bring the desire of the individual to the surface and the goals within his grasp.

Our coach, without ever giving it a second thought, is able to listen and hear what a person is saying aloud, while at the same time listen and hear what you're not saying. This is such an important quality because it comes at a time too many people are listening to you, but not hearing you.

It's a fact that we all need someone. It's that need that helps us build faith in ourselves which eventually enables us to grow and mature. Through knowing our coach, you are not alone. In times of stress and difficulty you're able to meet your challenges through his quiet compassion and wisdom. Our coach teaches you to give of yourself and understand those who succeed and falter. Our coach is serious but teaches you not to take yourself too seriously.

In just knowing our coach, Francis Cretzmeyer, it can be the foundation of knowledge and a young person's stepping stone to the future.

A TRACKMAN

The Six-Pack

The 1969-70 Iowa basketball team was one of my all-time favorites. Ralph Miller was the coach and the players liked to run and gun. I think they passed and shot the ball better than any other Iowa team. Also, they were excellent free throw shooters. They still remain the highest scoring team in Big Ten history, having averaged 102 points a game even before the three point shot was in effect. They had a perfect 14-0 record in the Big Ten, and won 17 of their last 18 games. The team was given the nickname "Six Pack" because six players played most of the minutes and scored most of the points. John Johnson and "Downtown" Fred Brown starred on the team and had long and successful NBA careers.

Photo Courtesy of Mark Wilson

The Six-Pack L to R: Fred Brown, Glenn Vidnovic, John Johnson, Dick Jensen, Ben McGilmer, and Chad Calabria

Murph Remembers...

Decade Six | 1973-1982

Decade 6: "Murph remembers..."

Starting the Johnson County I-Club

In 1973 the first meetings of the Johnson County I-Club were held. The original Johnson County I-Club organizers were Bud Suter, Dick McKeen, Bump Elliott and me. We most likely would have started our I-Club years earlier, but Forest Evashevski was opposed to the idea of a Johnson County I-Club, because he thought it might become too powerful and end up having the ability to select Iowa coaches. When Bump Elliott came on board as Athletic Director he saw the benefit of having an I-Club organization in the Iowa City area.

In 1974, when I became the club's second president, I had an idea that I believed would really get some spirit and energy into the early Friday morning breakfasts. These breakfasts were started in 1973 and held before the home football games. I wanted to have some members of the Iowa Marching Band and the Iowa Cheerleaders come and participate at the event. I wanted Iowa fans celebrating and shouting, "It's Great to be a Hawkeye!"

So, the Monday before the first Friday breakfast in 1974, I went to the Highlander Supper Club to meet with Bob McGurk. The breakfasts took place at the Highlander and McGurk was a co-owner. I wanted him to okay my idea. I showed up at his office and asked if we could have ten members of the Iowa marching band come to the Friday breakfasts. He said "NO". He felt the band would be too loud and that the guests in the motel would be disturbed by the music.

I wasn't ready to accept his answer. So, I went home and got my son, Joe's 'boom box' and came back to McGurk's office. He said, "You just don't give up, do you?" We tested the sound and McGurk realized the music would be okay and said, "Murph, you WIN, you can get ten band members!"

Jim Galiher got the band members and I think he was thrilled to death to do it.

I kept my idea quiet for the rest of the week, and excitedly waited for the big event. About 6:15 the morning of the breakfast I saw Bud Callahan from the athletic department come in the door at the Highlander. I went over and told him, "We GOT the band!" He was just as excited, as I was when I told him the band members and cheerleaders were just down the hall in a private room. I told him that he would have the job to open the door and let the band in on my signal once I started the meeting.

At 6:30 the crowd of about 600 began getting their breakfast and filing into the dining area. At 7:00 I gave Callahan the signal and the band and cheerleaders invaded the breakfast room playing "The Iowa Fight Song". The crowd went ape! It was great! It was one of the most exciting things I ever arranged.

The football coaches always attended the breakfasts too. Frank Lauterbur, Bob Commings, Hayden Fry and Kirk Ferentz have all come and addressed the crowd about that weekend's game during their tenure as head coach.

The pep band and cheer squad really livened up the breakfasts from 1974 thru 2014. Starting in 2015, due to a change to morning football practices, the breakfasts are being replaced by a new tradition of Friday lunches and pep rallies.

This photo shows a group of Iowa City Hawkeye fans discussing the idea of starting the Johnson County I-Club.

L to R Moe Whitebook, Earle Murphy, John Graham, John Winnie, Roland Smith

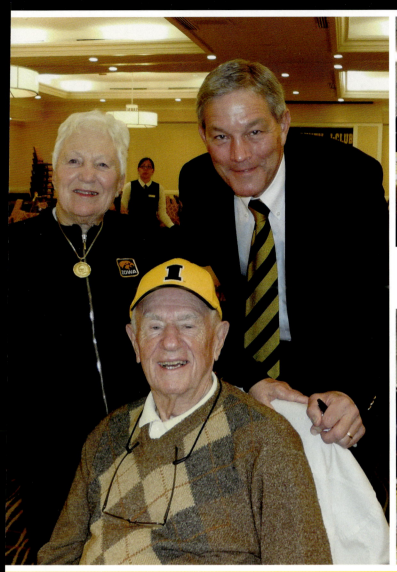

Left: Louise, Kirk Ferentz and Murph
Above: Bump, Darrell and Murph
Below: Murph, Louise and the Iowa Band

Another I-Club Event -- Alex Karras and the Old Gold Banquet

Some of our events hadn't had the attendance I expected. So, I had a team of about ten people call and invite all of the 600 people who showed up. We discovered people really needed to have a personal invitation to these events. I know they are glad they came, because this was a fantastic night!

Early in the evening, I got up and said: "Alex Karras will be tonight's guest of honor. Many of you have come and asked me what it cost to get Alex here tonight. Well that's simple. I just wiped out his bill at Bremers! And Alex said, "Murphy, you son of a bitch!" And the party was on! We had Cornish game hens for dinner, and Alex joked that "this is the smallest chicken I've ever seen!"

Photo Courtesy of Mark Wilson

Alex Karras at Iowa

Mark Wilson, Alex Karras, Earle Murphy,
Head Coach Bob Commings
Johnson County I-Club event in 1975

Murph Remembers...

Johnson County I-Club Presidents

The Johnson County I-Club board of directors consists of 36 members who promote, support, and raise money for University of Iowa athletic scholarships, building campaigns, etc. I've loved being involved and helped start the I-Club breakfasts, which are now being replaced by luncheons and pep rallies. I was President in 1974–1975, and my son John, was President in 1999–2000.

Dick McKeen, with the assistance of Bud Suter, and approval from Bump Elliott, started the Johnson County I-Club in 1972. Thanks to all of the board members who have served thru the years. Here is a list of Johnson County I-Club Presidents.

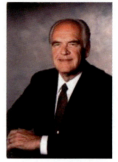

Dick McKeen

Name	Year	Name	Year
Dick McKeen	1972-73	Skip Wells	1994-95
Dick McKeen	1973-74	Wade Jones	1995-96
Earle Murphy	1974-75	Matt Pacha	1996-97
Jim Galiher	1975-76	Pat Harney	1997-98
Pat McCarney	1976-77	Dick Villhauer	1998-99
Moe Whitebook	1977-78	John Murphy	1999-00
Paul McKeen	1978-79	Tim Putney	2000-01
Bob Rasley	1979-80	Steve Droll	2001-02
John Lind	1980-81	Tom Kriz	2002-03
Ken Printen, MD	1981-82	Joe Wegman	2003-04
Gary Hughes	1982-83	Jeff Duncan	2004-05
Ted Pacha	1983-84	Wade Shriver	2005-06
Don Kirchner	1984-85	Roy Browning	2006-07
Dick Malcolm	1985-86	Chad Reimers	2007-08
Gary Pacha	1986-87	Eric Upchurch	2008-09
Garry Hamdorf	1987-88	Ted Sueppel	2009-10
Paul Maske	1988-89	Bob Bedford	2010-11
Pat Foster	1989-90	Anne Suter	2011-12
Chuck Traw	1990-91	Gary Vogt	2012-13
Mike Connell	1991-92	Scott Pantel	2013-14
Tim Krall	1992-93	George Karr	2014-15
Ron O'Neil	1993-94	Tom Robinson	2015-16
		Jim Conard	2016-17

Disneyland with the Girls

Tom Spalj was an amazing athletic trainer for the University of Iowa's sports programs. Tom and his wife Nancy, had made plans to buy the house directly to the east of our home. Sadly, we discovered that Tom was very sick from congenital problems. He died quickly after his diagnosis in 1972 at the age of 42. His wife Nancy and her son, Tom and daughter, Susan were forced to make other plans.

After his death, I promised Nancy that Louise and I would take her on a trip and just do something fun. In September of 1973, we flew to Los Angeles to attend the football game against UCLA. This was just our second game of the season, and it was our new football coach, Frank Lauterbur's second season. His wife Mary had invited Nancy to stay with her in her hotel room since Frank was in a suite of rooms and needed to be with the other coaches.

Nancy got in touch with us after Louise and I had settled into our room and she said that Mary wanted us to come up to their room to watch TV. The highly hyped tennis match between Billie Jean King and Bobbie Riggs was on. It had been billed as "The Battle of the Sexes". While we were watching the match, room service brought up a liquor delivery. Mary told the guy to bring it over to us. We thought that some Iowa fan had probably sent it up for Frank. We started drinking Frank's booze and Louise and I ask Nancy what she would like to do the next day. Mary asked if she could come along and of course I said, "yes" real quick.

Mary called me the *Boss*. I told them that I was the *Tour Leader*. Mary said that all of the women would do what I decided. But, when I said we were all going to Disneyland she protested. She didn't want to do a touristy, circus type of thing. She didn't think it would be any fun. Well, we convinced her to go. She had a ball and we could hardly drag her away from it.

Nancy watched a bear sleeping and snoring at Disneyland and she said that it sounded just like Tom. I said he's probably watching over us. And we had a good laugh. We had such fun and really had a great time.

September 22, 1973 Iowa played UCLA and lost the game 55-18. Disneyland might have been a high point that season, as we went on to lose every game. It was also Frank's last season as the head coach.

Dave Triplett

Dave Triplett was an all state football player from Des Moines Dowling. He played wide receiver for Iowa, graduating in 1972. He was one of my favorite players and we became good friends. Our children really enjoyed being around Dave. He would point to their shirt and say "You spilled something", they would look down to see, and he'd flick their chin with his finger. They loved it! Louise and I were honored to attend Dave's wedding in Davenport, where he married his wife Mary Ann.

At a young age, Dave was named the head football coach at Sioux City Heelan high school. He quickly led them to the 1975 Class 4A State Championship. He coached at the University of South Dakota from 1979 to 1988, where he compiled a nice record of 70-45. Three of his sons, Rory, Sean, and Tim all played football at South Dakota. Dave was an assistant football coach at Iowa from 1989 to 1995, before taking a leadership position with the UI Foundation.

Bobby Elliott, Brandt Yocum, and the new coat

Bobby Elliott was in college and playing for the Iowa football team in the mid 1970's. He lived in an old house on South Johnson Street with several teammates, including Dan McCarney, Brandt Yocum, and Rick Penney.

Bobby came into Bremers looking for a new winter jacket. He wanted something warm and dressy and I sold him a beautiful new Lakeland coat. He took it back to his house on the hanger and in a garment bag. He hung it up in the closet and went out to run a quick errand.

Brandt Yocum was home at the time and noticed how much Bobby liked his new coat. When Bobby returned, he sees Brandt lying on the couch with his big, hairy, shedding dog on top of him, and Bobby's new coat draped over the dog. Bobby Elliott went crazy. Brandt Yocum was quite the prankster. I can see it happening and it still makes me laugh.

What do Dave Triplett and Bobby Elliott have in common?

Dave Triplett (1972) and Bobby Elliott (1976) both were Big 10 Medal of Honor winners. The award goes to one student-athlete from each graduating class from each university who had "attained the greatest proficiency in athletics and scholastic work." An esteemed honor for two great Hawkeyes!

A poem written about Coach Bob Commings, by attorney Ed Rate.

I really liked it.

Ode to a Coach
by
Attorney Ed Rate
1974

There was a cocky fellow
With a shiny bald head
Came over from Ohio
"What a fool," they all said.

He hustled over Iowa
Put on quite a campaign
He talked pretty fast
And he talked pretty plain.

He spoke of the records
Of the team he had led
"Ho, ho, ho!" they all laughed
"That's what Lauterbur said!"

So they called Mr. Foerstner
And George agreed
A big name coach
Is what we need.

So they scoured the country
They worked very hard
But the big shot coaches all replied:
"No, no, not us, from your old graveyard!"

So the board brought in
The grassy guy
And said: We've decided,
To give you a try."

But for just one year,
You understand,
And you ain't walkin' away
With no fifty grand!"

So the coach took over
Without any more noise,
And started sorting out
The men from the boys.

He dredged up a man
By the name of Fick,
'Twas a four-letter word
But the kid was quick.

And they got together
A bunch of guys
Short of experience,
A little small in size.

But they had the guts
The coach gave them desire
And before we knew it,
The whole state was on fire,

You all know the rest
So have no fear,
I give you Bob Commings
The *Coach of the Yea*r!

Coach Bob Commings Sr discusses game strategy with his son, quarterback Bob Commings Jr. Iowa beat Iowa State 12-10 in 1977

The Kid and The Coach discuss strategy during Iowa's 12-10 victory over Iowa State Saturday at Kinnick Stadium

The recruitment of John Harty

John Harty was a big time defensive lineman recruit from Sioux City, Iowa in the mid 1970's. Bob Commings, Bill Whisler, Louise and I flew over to visit John. I had met him earlier on one of his visits to Iowa City. Nebraska was a national power and John was trying to decide between playing football for Iowa or Nebraska.

Head Coach Bob Commings promised John that if he committed to the Hawkeyes, he could sign his letter of intent in the office of Governor Robert Ray at the State Capitol.

That's exactly what happened and it was a very unique situation. As a matter of fact, I think it drew a hand slap from the NCAA for some type of minor infraction.

John Harty had a great career at Iowa and graduated in 1980. He was drafted in the second round by the San Francisco 49ers, and was a Super Bowl Champion.

Who would have the guts to steal the cap of Woody Hayes?

Woody Hayes was a legendary football coach for the Ohio State. He coached the Buckeyes for 28 years, from 1951 through 1978, and was inducted into the College Football Hall of Fame. His teams won five national championships and 13 Big Ten titles.

He served in the US Navy in World War II, and rose to the rank Lieutenant Commander. Woody was a tough, fiery, and hot tempered coach. On December 29th, 1978 his career ended in disgrace after he struck a player during the Gator Bowl. In the final minutes of a 17-15 loss, Charlie Bauman of Clemson intercepted an Ohio State pass. As he was running out of bounds, a frustrated Woody Hayes stepped up and punched him. The next day, he was fired. After his firing, Hayes reflected on his career and said, "Nobody despises losing more than I do. That got me in trouble over the years, but it also has made a man of mediocre ability into a pretty good coach."

On October 15th, 1977, Woody Hayes and his Buckeyes beat the Iowa Hawkeyes 27-6. Mike Gatens was watching the end of the game from the sidelines, and a friend told him to steal Woody's cap. Without giving it much thought, he sprinted to midfield as Woody Hayes and Bob Commings were shaking hands. Gatens, who played basketball at Iowa, is 6' 8" tall, and easily picked the black OSU cap off his head. The normally aggressive Coach Hayes did not attempt to chase him down. Gatens ran over to the sideline where an OSU student manager asked him to give it back. Mike declined the request, jumped the railing, ran up to an exit, and escaped out of Kinnick Stadium.

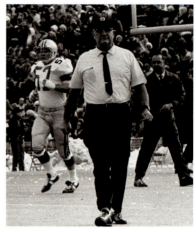

The next day, on the front page of a Columbus, Ohio newspaper, there were four pictures recapping the theft of Woody's cap. A photographer had taken them from the press box. As Mike reflected on his improper behavior, he decided to mail Woody Hayes five dollars to pay for the cap, along with a letter about how impressed he was with his football teams. Woody sent Mike back a nice letter thanking him for his integrity, and informed him that since the cap belonged to the school, the money was donated to the OSU Foundation. So unintentionally, the Iowa Basketball Letterman made a donation to Ohio State, but it made Mike feel better about ownership of his new prized possession.

There were stories written about the theft in the Iowa City Press Citizen, and also in the "Scorecard" section of Sports Illustrated. One of my favorite articles was titled "Thief with Class", because Mike had paid for the cap. That Christmas, Julie Gatens gave her husband a beautiful box frame with his letter to Woody, his letter back to Mike, some newspaper articles, and in the middle of the frame... the infamous cap. Each year during the week of the Ohio State game, the box frame hangs on display in a local restaurant.

Photo Courtesy of Mike Gatens

Decade Six | 1973-1982

The cap caper begins with Gatens, dressed in black with sunglasses, removing the cap from the head of Coach Woody Hayes. Top right, team manager for Ohio State witnesses theft and begins chase. Bottom, Coach Bob Commings running across the field for postgame handshake.

Chase continues…Buckeye manager in hot pursuit and closing in.

Almost apprehended…state patrol standing by… throws the cap to Iowa fan in the stands to divert attention… jumps the railing into stands… gets the cap tossed back to him.

Photos Courtesy of Mike Gatens

Makes clean getaway…infamous cap in right hand.

The Mike Gatens "McDonalds" game

Lute Olson's first year as the Iowa basketball coach was during the 1974-1975 season. Some of the players on Lute's first team were Bruce "Sky" King, Dan Frost, Larry Moore, Larry Parker, Scott Thompson, Fred Haberecht, and Mike Gatens.

On January 11, 1975, the Hawkeyes had a road game with the Indiana Hoosiers. Indiana was loaded with talent. They were so dominant that four of their starters would make the five-man All-Big Ten first team. Those players were Scott May, Kent Benson, Quinn Buckner, and Steve Green.

On that night in Bloomington, the Hoosiers were pounding the Hawkeyes, as they often did to their opponents that year. With a few seconds left in the game, Indiana led Iowa 104-48. Mike Gatens was fouled and went to the line for two free throws. We all know that Indiana is a basketball school with very loyal and rabid fans. With this score, you would think most fans around the country would be heading to the exits, but all 17,500 Hoosier fans were still there. They were cheering loud and going crazy as Gatens took his first foul shot. He missed it, and the arena went nuts with celebration! Gatens made his next free throw, making the final score 104-49. The Hawkeyes left the court depressed by the final score and confused by the crowd behavior those final seconds.

After the players showered and changed clothes, Kent Benson, Indiana's All-American center came up to Mike Gatens in the hallway. He asked Mike if he wanted a handful of ticket stubs. Mike asked him what the deal was with the ticket stubs. Kent explained that when Indiana scores more than 100 points, the local McDonalds restaurants give every ticket holder a free drink. If Indiana held an opponent under 50 points, they got a free order of French fries also. And if they did both in the same game, they got a full meal, a hamburger, french fries, and a drink. That explained the huge cheer from the crowd after the missed free throw.

Needless to say, Gatens declined the ticket stubs. To make an ugly night even worse, the team got stuck in traffic on the way to the airport due to the long line of cars backed up at every McDonalds. Years later, Gatens says he looks at the positive side of the story, and remembers it as a night when one of his missed free throws threw a dinner party for 17,500 Indiana basketball fans.

Mike Gatens attended the Big Ten basketball tournament a few years ago in Indianapolis. He was in a sports bar and started talking with some elderly Indiana fans. He asked them if they remembered the game in 1975 when Indiana beat Iowa 104-49 and every ticket holder received a free burger, fries, and drink. They told him yes they did remember and some of them had been at the game. Mike explained that it was his missed free throw that bought them all dinner at McDonalds. They all had a good laugh, and Mike finally received something in return for that fateful night. The Indiana fans bought him a drink!

Some of My Town Hawk Experiences

I was a Town Hawk. I really enjoyed helping bring players to Iowa and encouraging them to become a Hawkeye. I was one of about 30 Hawkeye supporters who spent time with the recruits both in Iowa City and in their hometowns. While I was a Town Hawk the NCAA had much more lenient rules on recruiting. Once our recruits became a Hawkeye they also became members of our families; we brought them into our homes. I became a Town Hawk for Andre Tippett, Norman Granger, and Keith Hunter. They all became Iowa Football captains.

In the spring of 1980, I went with Hayden Fry, Bernie Wyatt, and Barry Alvarez to New Jersey. We flew in a private plane on recruiting trip. Hayden asked me to go to Barrington High School. Barrington had a mostly black student body, and it was a tough school. I had to press a button to open the door, and then a police guard let me go through the metal detectors. It was a new experience for me. I was told where to meet Norman and Keith. I asked Norman who was after him, and he said, "Penn State". Keith didn't have anybody recruiting him. We talked for a while and then Norman asked me to go to a high school basketball game with him. The games were in the afternoon, and as I was watching the game I commented to Norman that the refs were being unfair and 'doing a number' on them. I noticed that Norman went courtside at half time. He pointed up to me in the stands as he was talking to the refs. When he returned I asked him what that was all about. He said, I told them, "Whitey says you're hosing us." I watched more of the second half and then became nervous and didn't want to stay for the rest of the game. I told Norman that I wanted him to call me a cab. I knew I needed to get to New York City, and fast. I was worried that there might be trouble once the game was over. The cab came and the driver says he won't take me to my hotel. He can't leave New Jersey and drive the bridge into New York City because he's not licensed to drive his cab over the river. So, I tell him the story and he tells me to get in. He really saved my life and got me safely to New York City.

I went on to New York City to work with some clothiers to prepare Bremers for our new fall lines. I stayed at the Warwick Hotel.

Norman did come to Iowa and he was a four-time Iowa letterman at fullback for the Hawkeyes. He was Iowa's co-captain in both 1982 and 1983 and was voted the team's Co-Most Valuable Player in 1983. He played pro ball for the Dallas Cowboys and the Atlanta Falcons.

Keith Hunter was interested in Pittsburgh, Syracuse, or Penn State. But he chose Iowa because it was different from the East Coast and he liked the fact that there was less crime. Keith came to Iowa and played football from 1981-1984. He was a cornerback and lettered all four years. He was the Iowa Co-Captain in 1984. He played pro ball for the Cleveland Browns.

Andre Tippett

Iowa Hawkeye All-American and Pro Football Hall of Fame Inductee.

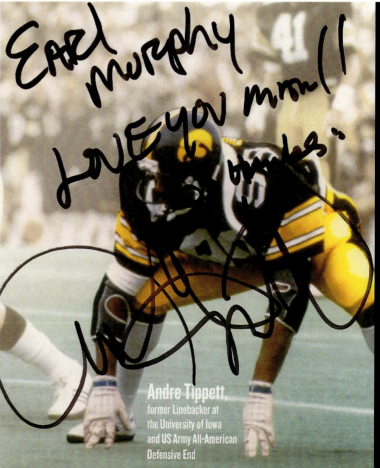

Andre Tippett, former Linebacker at the University of Iowa and US Army All-American Defensive End

University of Iowa "Town Hawks" group photo, 1974.
The Town Hawks would take football recruits to lunch and talk to them about Iowa City and the University of Iowa.

Front Row: Head Football Coach Bob Commings
Row 1, L to R: Doug Goodfellow, Pat Foster, Burt Frantz, Moe Whitebook, Ralph Radcliff, Bob Rasley, Don Kirchner.
Row 2, L to R: Earl Yoder, Bob Dotson, Earle Murphy, John Krieger, Dave Clark, Bill Stoddard, John Loughran.
Row 3, L to R: Pat McCarney, Jim Galiher, Terry Tegen, Harve Garner, Paul McKeen, Tom Nereim
Row 4, L to R: Marty Sixt, Dr. Fred Riddle, Jerry Seifert, John Lind, Dick McKeen, Gary Slager.

Andre Tippett was also from Barrington High School. He started his collegiate football career at Ellsworth College in Iowa Falls in 1978. Andre became a Hawkeye football player in 1979 as a defensive end. Andre would visit me at Bremers and sometimes come to the house. He played for three years under Hayden Fry and he was often a problem for opposing quarterbacks. Andre was first-team all-Big Ten his junior and senior years. He played pro ball for the New England Patriots in the 1980's and was a five time Pro Bowler and a two time First-Team All-Pro. He was inducted into the NFL Hall of Fame in 2008.

Andre was in Iowa City for the Iowa-Wisconsin game in 2013. I was so excited when I learned that he was signing autograph cards at the south end of Kinnick Stadium before the game. My daughter Ann had been exploring the different tailgating venues, and she had spoken with Andre. He was really interested in seeing me. So, my son John and Ann and I headed off in a golf cart to find him. He was still signing autographs, but when he saw me, he stopped and came over and gave me a hug and kissed my cheek. We were so happy to see one another. The bonds we made have lasted over the years.

Treye Jackson was a running back from Newton, Iowa. He was being recruited by Hayden Fry in 1980. He was also being recruited by Oklahoma, Nebraska, and Alabama. I was his Town Hawk and ready to host his Iowa City visit. He was with Dan McCarney, the defensive line coach and they were traveling in Roy Carver's private plane. Treye asked the pilot to fly around Iowa City twice so he could really see what the town looked like. He visited me and our family and toured Iowa City and the campus. He decided to play football for Iowa.

During the game in 1981 he caught the "Amen" touchdown pass thrown by Chuck Long. The team goes wild on the sidelines, and we won the game. He became an Iowa Letterman in 1982. In 1983 he felt he wasn't being played enough and transferred to Colorado State.

Decade Six | 1973-1982

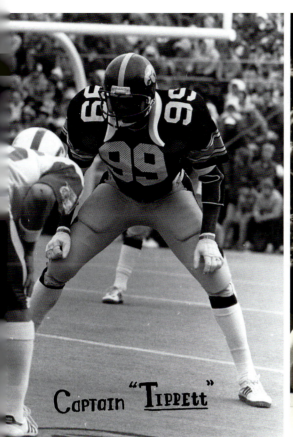
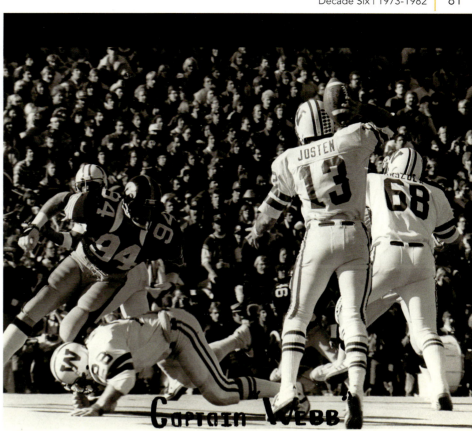

Defensive Co-Captains 1981 - Andre Tippett, Brad Webb
Two of my favorites!

Andre Tippett and Murph before a Hawkeye football game

1980 Carver Hawkeye Arena Fundraising Drive

I was involved in the campaign to raise money to build Carver-Hawkeye arena. Jim Scanlon had given me a check for $25,000 that I delivered to the office of my fundraising team leader. The check was placed on a cluttered desk and ended up missing. I was relieved when it was finally found about a month later. The fundraiser was a huge success, and Carver-Hawkeye Arena opened in 1983.

Photo Courtesy of John Murphy

Which Iowa athlete scored the first team points in Carver-Hawkeye arena?

No, it wasn't Bobby Hansen or Greg Stokes. The first athlete to score points in Carver-Hawkeye arena was Tim Riley. On January 3rd 1983, the Iowa Hawkeye wrestling team beat the Oklahoma Sooners 35-7. Riley, an Iowa City native and All-American wrestler, won the first match in the new arena.

Jim Hayes

In the fall of 1981, Jim Hayes and I took a small plane to Ann Arbor, Michigan, to attend an Iowa-Michigan football game. Jim's a good friend and a prominent Iowa City attorney. We were in the hotel room when Jim got a phone call from his law office. I left the room and went down to the hotel lobby. After his phone call, Jim found me and said "Don't say anything to anybody, but I just won a lawsuit worth more than a million dollars."

We got into the line at the busy hotel bar, and Jim Zabel and Bob Brooks were standing there. Never being one to follow instructions, I told them that Hayes just won a lawsuit worth over a million dollars. Zabel shouts out, that's great, he can buy us a drink!" Jim Hayes had a good laugh, bought some drinks, and enjoyed every minute of the evening.

The next day I had a unique opportunity presented to me before the game. KCJJ Radio station owner Kent Braverman asked me to do the color commentary for their broadcast. I agreed to help out and it was a great experience. Tom Nichols kicked three field goals and the Hawkeyes upset the favored Wolverines 9-7.

Years ago, Jim Hayes purchased the house in Iowa City where famous artist Grant Wood once lived. It's a beautiful home on Court Street and Jim has done a great job remodeling and decorating the historic property. As kind and generous as I've always known Jim to be, it doesn't surprise me that he's donating the house to the University of Iowa and the School of Art and Art History.

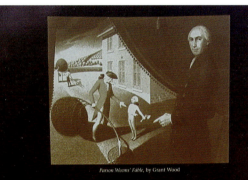

Parson Weems' Fable, by Grant Wood

"1142"

"1142" was what Grant Wood, one of America's most celebrated regional artists, fondly called the home where he lived for the last seven years of his life. He bought "1142" in 1935, following the tremendous success of his painting *American Gothic* and his subsequent appointment to the Art faculty of the University of Iowa. The Anamosa native was a skilled craftsman as well as a painter, and spent the next two years extensively remodeling the house himself, inside and out, even designing and building furniture. Wood planted the junipers on the eastern lot line and created the current retaining wall out of Stone City limestone. He also rescued most of the original shutters, which a previous resident had fashioned into chicken coops behind the house, and restored them to their present condition. Although Wood's studio was in the loft of the carriage house, now the pool house/guest house, he painted the satiric *Parson Weems' Fable* in what is currently the master bedroom.

Nicholas Oakes, a brickmaker from Ohio, designed this Italianate-style home for his family and constructed it of bricks from his brickworks, 200 yards to the south. (*See* The Oakes Brickworks, *reverse*.) "1142" was completed in 1858. More widely known as the Grant Wood House, it was placed on the National Register of Historic Places in 1978 and was named an Iowa City landmark in 1996.

John Alt

In the 1980's I was John Alt's Town Hawk. Coach Dan McCarney was recruiting him. John lived in Columbia Heights, a suburb of Minneapolis, Minnesota. He was a terrific high school athlete and earned All-State honors in both football and basketball. John was heavily recruited and Iowa really wanted him as he was 6'7" and weighed about 240 pounds.

John was making his official Iowa visit. Dan asked John if he would like to visit with me, but John became nervous on the plane because they tried to call me and the phone didn't work. This was his first airplane trip and he was worried that something was wrong with the plane. It landed safely, and he lived! The first thing he did in Iowa City was to come and visit with me. In my role as a Town Hawk I shared all of the benefits he would enjoy by coming to Iowa. We had a great time and he decided to come to Iowa to play ball. John became a friend of the Murphy family, too.

Near the end of his sophomore year Spring Practice was just about to begin. John comes into Bremers, obviously upset. "I want to talk to you," he said. He followed me upstairs into the office and closed the door. Before that, we had never closed the office door. John said, "They want to move me to inside!" That meant Coach Fry wanted him to play left tackle. He was very upset, as he wanted to play tight end and score touchdowns.

I listened to John talk for awhile and then I said, "John, go back and talk to Coach Fry. You need to think about what's good for the team and for the fans." I told him he wouldn't make a cent at tight end in the pros, but at offensive tackle he'd make a million dollars. John became one of the greatest tackles in Iowa history, and grew to 6'8" and 300 pounds.

> "This is what an offensive tackle looks like."

In 1984, the Kansas City Chiefs drafted John in the 1st round. When he was offered his pro contract he got a million dollar signing bonus! He became an All Pro tackle and was inducted into the Kansas City Chiefs Hall of Fame in 2002.

He's quite a guy.

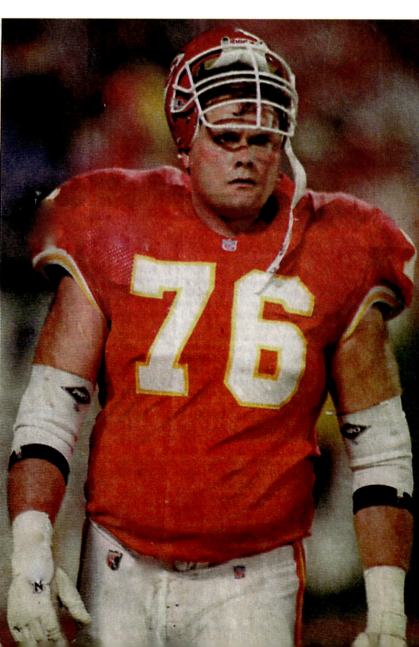

NCAA Shirt Sale Concern of 1982

Iowa was having a great basketball season and Bremers had special ordered yellow t-shirts with black letters for the player's names and numbers, like Boyle #40. We had sold a ton of these shirts and Bump found out about it and asked me to stop.

He called and told me to expect a letter explaining the NCAA rules on selling player merchandise. Bump said he knew I would abide by the letter. So, and Bump didn't know this, before the letter arrived, I called the manufacturer and asked if they still had our order. I said I would like to order 12 dozen more!

Boy, did those shirts ever sell! Once the letter came, I didn't order any more shirts.

THE UNIVERSITY OF IOWA

Intercollegiate Athletics

ATHLETIC OFFICE BUILDING
IOWA CITY, IOWA 52242

February 15, 1982

Mr. Earl Murphy
Bremers
120 East Washington
Iowa City, Iowa   52240

Dear Earl:

It has come to my attention that you have on display and for sale yellow Tee shirts with black numbers and names of members of our basketball team. This concerned me in light of recent legislation which prevents athletes giving permission for their names to be used in this manner and further that affirmative action must be taken if the situation should arise. I contacted Bill Hunt, Assistant Executive Director of the NCAA, so that he might clarify this for me and he cited Case 39 (copy enclosed) of the NCAA Manual. It clearly states that this practice is not permissible.

I, with this letter, am taking affirmative action in requesting that you discontinue displaying for sale Tee shirts with the numbers and names of members of our basketball team.

I am well aware that you would do nothing to jeopardize our program and your consideration and cooperation will be very much appreciated.

Sincerely,

C. W. Elliott
Director

P

Bobby Knight and Bump Elliott

Bump and Barbara Elliott invited Louise and I to an Iowa - Indiana basketball game at the old Fieldhouse. We were seated in the east bleachers, ten rows up. It was a very heated game and the score volleyed back and forth. Iowa played hard and won the game. When there were just about 30 seconds left and the score 80-79, Bump leans over and tells me he is going to go courtside in case there's a riot.

But, before he gets there, the game ends. He meets Bobby Knight at courtside just as Bobby is leaving the game and says, "Nice game, Bobby." Bobby stares at him and replies, "F... Y..!"

Bump returns to his seat and his face is a really deep red. I ask him what happened. He said nothing had happened, "Why?" But I told him that his face was really red, and again asked what happened? He said, "Do you know what Bobby Knight just said to me?" Bump replayed the short exchange he had with Bobby. I was amazed. Thirty years ago, language like this was hardly ever used, and Bobby's swearing was really disturbing. I asked Bump what he was going to do about it. Bump told me he would go into work at eight o'clock the next morning and wait for Bobby to call him. He figured he'd call at about 8:30 or 9:00.

The next morning, I waited to make sure I wasn't interrupting, and then called Bump about 11:00. I was really interested in finding out what happened. Bump told me Bobby had called and apologized. Bobby had said, "I'm sorry." And Bump said, "Okay." I thanked Bump and hung up. I just wanted to know how the story ended.

The Pink Paint Job

Every time a team comes to Iowa to play football there is discussion about the visitor's locker room and its pink color scheme. Some say Hayden Fry and his study of human psychology understood pink to be a calming color, which would keep the opponent from getting keyed up for the game. According to this account, Hayden deliberately had the locker room painted pink.

My conversation with Bump Elliott gives a different insight. Bump, who was the Iowa Athletic Director, wanted to paint the east locker room in Kinnick Stadium, the opponent's dressing room. He asked Gary Kurdelmeier to go to the general store and buy some paint. When Gary arrived at the store he discovered that the only paint they had in stock was PINK! Gary called Bump and explained the situation. Bump said, "If pink is all they've got, we'll put that on!"

So it was painted pink.

I love this cartoon done by Frank Miller for the Des Moines Register on January 1, 1982
It appears the father time is a Hawkeye fan!

Taffy Apple Murphy

I had just won $50.00 from a raffle held at Regina.

The next day Jerry Hilgenberg came into the store and said his Dad "Curly" Hilgenberg was coming to town with five newborn puppies. Jerry asked me if I wanted to buy one. He told me Forrest Evashevski's dog was the father and his Dad's dog was the mother of the litter.

I told him we could not have a dog because my wife Louise was allergic to dog hair. He said that poodles have fur and she would be fine. I asked Jerry how much they wanted for a puppy and he said $50.00. So I decided to buy a family dog with my raffle winnings.

My son Jeff and I went over to see the five puppies. I asked him which one he liked and he said "all of them". He picked out a caramel brown female we named Taffy Apple.

Louise and I and our seven children really enjoyed the 18 years that Taffy was our family dog. Of course as a loyal Hawkeye fan, it was neat to have a dog that was 50% Evashevski and 50% Hilgenberg.

Mary Sue Murphy and Taffy in 1983

Herky the Hawk History

Iowa is the Hawkeye State! The name was popularized in the book "The Last of the Mohicans," written in 1826 by James Fenimore Cooper. A hero in the fictional novel was named Hawkeye. The Delaware Indians bestowed the name on a white scout, who lived and hunted with them. **Hawkeye was strong, astute, resourceful, and feared by his opponents.**

The two men most responsible for the promotion of the Hawkeye nickname were Judge David Rorer of Burlington and newspaper publisher James Edwards of Fort Madison. Judge Rorer suggested "The Hawkeye State" after finding the name in the famous novel. Burlington was established in 1833, after the Black Hawk War of 1832. Mr. Edwards moved his newspaper to Burlington and renamed it *The Hawk-Eye* and *Iowa Patriot*, in tribute to his friend Chief Black Hawk, who lived his final years in present day eastern Iowa. Territorial officials gave the Hawkeye nickname their formal approval in 1838. From 1838 to 1840, Burlington was the capital of the Iowa Territory. Iowa City then served as the territorial capital from 1840 to 1846. Iowa officially became a state in 1846, and Iowa City became the first state capital of Iowa. The University of Iowa was founded in 1847.

In 1948, a Hawk cartoon character was created by UI journalism instructor Dick Spencer. The UI Athletic Department held a contest to name the character. John Franklin, an alumnus from Belle Plaine, IA, suggested **the winning entry of "Herky" as a reference to the Greek God "Hercules."** Herky the Hawk first appeared as a costumed mascot during an Iowa football game in the 1950's.

Tiger Hawk History

After being hired in 1978, Hayden Fry wanted a new, distinctive decal on the football helmets. Sports Information Director George Wine contacted Charles Edwards, who worked for Pepco Litho, the company that printed media guides for the University of Iowa. Edwards turned to Bill Colbert, the art director for Three Arts Advertising in Cedar Rapids.

On a plane trip home from the Twin Cities, Colbert pulled out his pen and sketched out the rough design of what later becomes known as the Tiger Hawk, on a paper napkin. *"I wanted to design something that had the head, eye, and beak of the hawk. I wanted it to have simplicity, yet have a striking effect," said Colbert.* George Wine took two black helmets to Colbert and he placed

his gold Tiger Hawk decal on the sides of both helmets. On June 11, 1979, Wine, Edwards, and Colbert presented the newly decorated helmets to Hayden. He liked the new decal and approved the design.

Fry and Colbert formed the Hawkeye Marketing Group, and put the Tiger Hawk logo on caps, shirts, and numerous other items. When Colbert moved to Chicago in 1982, the University of Iowa licensed the Tiger Hawk and took over the ownership of the logo.

America Needs Farmers

In 1985, Hayden Fry created a simple but strong message by placing A-N-F stickers on the Iowa football helmets. The logo was noticed by thousands of fans and television viewers, and it promoted the importance of farming to a national audience. At the time, the state of Iowa was in the middle of a farm crisis, and nearly 20,000 family farms went under by the time it was over. Of course, many of our athletes grew up on Iowa farms or in farming communities, as did many of our Hawkeye fans and boosters. It was a great idea.

To this day, more than 30 years later, Kirk Ferentz and the Hawkeyes continue to show support to hard working Iowa farmers who are so important to the Iowa economy.

Thanks again Hayden. America Needs Farmers!

Murph Remembers...

Decade Seven | 1983-1992

"Murph remembers..."

Iowa Letterman

In 1984 I as elected an honorary member of the University of Iowa's National Lettermen's Club. I received a Lettermen's ring, and a blanket and membership in the honorary Lettermen's Club. For me, being an honorary Letterman has been an honor. I wear my ring with pride.

Pat McCarney, Charles Swisher, and Earle Murphy
Honorary Letterman Inductees 1984

Earl
Congratulations on being inducted as an honorary letterman for 1984. A recognition so well deserved & too long in coming.

Bill Snyder

Bill Snyder was Hayden Fry's offensive coordinator from 1979 to 1988. He left after 10 years at Iowa to become the head coach at Kansas State, where he's had a very successful coaching career. He's a class act and a good friend.

The National Lettermen's Club   Carver-Hawkeye Arena, Iowa City, Iowa 52242

June 4, 1984

Earl Murphy
1692 Ridge Road
Iowa City, Iowa 52240

Dear Earl,

It is my pleasant duty to inform you that the University of Iowa Lettermen's Club elected you as an honorary member at their June 2 meeting. It is a prestigious award that very few people have received.

You will be introduced at the Iowa/Iowa State football game at half time on September 8. That night you will be a guest of honor at the Lettermen's reunion banquet. You will be given the University of Iowa lettermen's blanket, ring and fully paid membership. An honorary letterman has all of the rights and privileges that any Iowa letterman has. I will be calling you with more information about the Lettermen's Club and more details on the September 8 week end.

Two other people were nominated as honorary lettermen with you. They are Patrick McCarney and Charles Swisher. We prefer to hold the newspaper release of your election to the Lettermen's Club until just before the lettermen's reunion. The information will not be secret as the Lettermen's Club meeting is open to the public and some peole already know it. I would appreciate a head and shoulders shot of yourself for the news media.

Again, congratulations. I cannot think of three more deserving people than those elected this year. You join an outstanding group of honoree lettermen.

Sincerely,

Gary Kurdelmeier

Gary Kurdelmeier
Executive Director

Murph Remembers...

Iowa Basketball

I have enjoyed Iowa basketball. Lute Olson was an intense coach, who could really get his players to play hard. During his tenure at Iowa from 1974-1983, the Hawks had a 168-90 overall win-loss record. Lute and I were friends.

Matt Gatens was recruited by Steve Alford to play basketball at Iowa. He played for Todd Lickliter, and Fran McCaffrey.

Matt ended his career as one of our all-time leading scorers. His talent, leadership, and perseverance make him one of my all-time favorites.

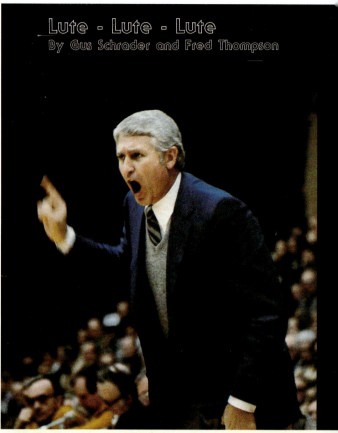

I am not sure why fans started repeating Lute's name three times; it was probably just fun to say. I liked getting the card from Lute where he repeated my name.

George Raveling
Iowa Basketball Coach 1983-1986

Bremers had a contract to fit and provide coats for the coaches on the basketball team when George Raveling was the head coach. Mark Walz, one of our salesmen, went over to measure the coaches and put in an order for nine coats. When he arrived George Raveling was busy on the telephone and didn't have time to have his measurements taken. So the next morning, Mark says "Murph, I'll see ya." And I said, "Where are you going?" He told me that he was going back to the athletic offices to measure Coach Raveling. I said, "Oh no, you are not going there, he is coming here. We filled our obligation to provide the service yesterday, and if he wants a coat he needs to come down here." So Mark called the office and explained that Murph was upset and what needed to happen. About two hours later George came walking into Bremers with a package under his arm. It was a black and white silhouette of a basketball game being played outside. He said, come on I want to give you a hug. He wanted to make everything okay.

The historic "I Have a Dream" speech is owned by George Raveling

George told me he was at the Lincoln Memorial in 1963 when Martin Luther King Jr. gave the famous "I Have a Dream" speech. He was working security near the stage and right after it was over, he asked Dr. King for his notes and he was handed the original copy. He quickly possessed three typed pages of what has become one of our nations most famous and historic speeches. I believe he currently keeps the papers in a vault at his bank. He has been offered over three million dollars for the speech. George says he has willed it to his children on the condition they not sell it. He's been quoted as saying, "The speech belongs to America. It would be sacrilegious of me to try to sell it or profit from it. Everything in life you can't equate to money."

When he moved away from Iowa City it was on a Sunday. Bump called and said, "Why don't you and Louise come down to the University Athletic Club and join us in saying goodbye to George." So Louise and I gladly joined Bump and his wife Barbara and George. The five of us laughed and had a great goodbye celebration. When we said our final goodbyes in the parking lot, I saw that Bump and George didn't shake hands, they hugged.

George is quite a guy.

Front L to R: Bernie Wyatt, Barry Alvarez, Bill Brashier, Dan McCarney, Bobby Stoops
Back L to R: Bill Snyder, Del Miller, Kirk Ferentz, Hayden Fry, Carl Jackson, Don Patterson, Bill Dervrich

One of the best coaching staffs ever assembled. Five College Football Hall of Fame coaches in Hayden Fry, Bill Snyder, Barry Alvarez…and some day…Kirk Ferentz and Bobby Stoops.

1983 Iowa Coaching Staff

L to R: Hap Peterson, Chuck Long, Mike Haight, Ronnie Harmon, Larry Station

1985 Iowa Co-Captains

Who's flying the plane?
The tuxedos were supplied by Bremers so I decided to join the photo!

#1 ranked Iowa defeated #2 ranked Michigan 12-10 with last second field goal in 1985

Photo courtesy of Bob Goodfellow

One of the most exciting finishes ever at Kinnick Stadium. On October 20th, 1985, with a Rob Houghtlin field goal on the final play of the game, our #1 ranked Iowa Hawkeyes defeated the #2 ranked Michigan Wolverines 12-10.

Barry Alvarez, Bryce Paup, and the Shrine Bowl

In 1986, Barry Alvarez, Kirk Ferentz and I went to the Iowa Shrine Bowl Game. It's a post season high school all-star game held in Cedar Falls. At the time, both Barry and Kirk were assistant coaches at Iowa.

I had a program, and during the game Barry asked, "Who is number 45?" I told him "His name is Bryce Paup and he is going to Northern Iowa."

Barry Said, "Damn, he's the best player on the field. He's going to be an All-American at UNI, play in the pros, and make a lot of money. You mark my word."

Barry was right. Bryce Paup went on to have a great college and professional career. He was the NFL Defensive Player of the Year in 1995, a four time Pro-Bowler, and he made a lot of money.

Every time I would see Barry Alvarez after that, instead of saying "Hi", he would say "Bryce Paup." And I'd say, "Bryce Paup." That's how we would greet each other.

Louise and I went to Chicago once for a Big Ten Football Media Day. There were about eleven booths and tables set up in a hotel conference room, all the same size. At each table there were a head coach and two players representing every Big Ten team. As we walked in, Barry Alvarez was getting interviewed by a television station. He was standing up there, and during this interview, he looks over and sees me, and raises his hand, and shouts out "Bryce Paup." I must have been about 50 feet away from him. Barry is a hell of a nice guy.

Introducing Hayden

by Louise Murphy

I was asked to introduce Coach Hayden Fry at an early morning I-Club breakfast during the 1987 football season. Following are my remarks made that morning:

"Good Morning. I may seem a little uncomfortable standing up here, but the truth is I have this mosquito bite in the middle of my back. I am trying very hard to practice self-control. But sometimes coach, you just can't scratch where it itches!"

Sounds of laughter erupted and I patted Hayden's shoulder. The more the people reacted, the more comfortable I felt.

"Since the men's I-Club has welcomed women's participation, it is my pleasure to be able to introduce Hayden Fry. You all know something about Coach, but did you ever realize as men and women we may have a different perception about Hayden... and someone yelled out, 'I sure hope so!'

"Men see him as a fine football coach, organized, competent and an excellent recruiter. Women on the other hand... I paused and smiled at Hayden... they see tall, and tan and handsome."

"I remember the first time I met Hayden Fry. It was a cold freezing December day and Murph and I were at a basketball game in the old, noisy Fieldhouse. As he was passing nearby in the crowd I said to Murph, "I want to meet him!" Murph introduced me and Hayden graciously extended his arm while bending down towards me and I felt the warmest, firmest handshake ever. And he kept looking at me all the time.

He said, "Mrs. Murphy, I've been looking forward to meeting you for a long time. This is indeed a pleasure." And... I BELIEVED HIM!!"

I waited while the crowd clapped, cheered and laughed. They were aware of his dynamic charisma too.

"Have you noticed, at banquets or during conversations, Hayden refers to himself as a, *poor old country boy*. Well I've thought about his Texan charm... and if this is a poor old country boy--- fly me south!"

"With humor, Hayden assured us that he is a country boy. He even has a plan for his gravestone. He says it will read, *"Here lies John Hayden Fry, the last of the poor old country boys"*. And further down, toward the bottom it will be engraved,
"Shirley, I told you I was sick."

"Obviously he has a beautiful wife and together they have built a lovely red tiled home north of Iowa City. It is tucked in the woods, isolated; so much that at 2:00am after a winning football game, they can hardly hear the sounds of a car horn honking the tune of the Iowa Fight song. But, I have had the experience of the late night horn sounding the Iowa Fight song in my backyard because a boy in the Iowa Marching Band lives right next door." (I smiled and pointed at Donny Hughes.)

"And so, Hayden is a fascinating, dynamic, complex man.
From a man's point of view... he's a winner!
From a woman's point of view...he's a REAL WINNER! May I introduce your coach, John Hayden Fry."

As Hayden approached the podium, I felt great because everyone seemed to really have enjoyed my introduction. Hayden handed me the notes I had forgotten and addresses the group, "I don't know how these breakfasts could be more enjoyable for me. And all this time I thought that 'Murph was the one' and then Louise comes forward! Thank you Louise."

After my introduction, Hap Peterson's mother came over to the head table, smiled and hugged me saying, "I know exactly how you feel." Her son was an All Big Ten nose guard on the football team, and as a football player's mother I'm sure she was also recruited!

Bill Quinby and the Big 10 "Coin Toss" Coin

My wife, Louise, was given a special gift from Bill Quinby. Bill was a Big Ten and NFL official and a friend of ours. The City of Cedar Rapids recently renamed a baseball field in his honor because of his tireless community volunteer efforts. Bill was also a recipient of the University of Iowa's Lifetime Achievement award.

Louise and I attended a party and we were talking with Bill about the University of Iowa and the new hospital wing that was being built around the existing tower. Louise told him she worked with medical students at the University's School of Medicine. Bill explained that his son was planning to go to medical school. But, he had been driving his car near the hospital construction zone and the heavy ball from one of the cranes swung into his car, killing him instantly. At that time there were no beeping or warning sounds on heavy equipment to alert drivers to their presence. This safeguard was put into effect as a result his tragic accident.

Bill was suddenly emotional and said to Louise, "I want you to have this in honor of my son." And he pulled the rare Big Ten coin out of his pocket.

He explained that at the end of the season, the winning team captain would get one of these coins. Bill had it because he was an official. These coins are scarce now, especially since more schools have joined the Big Ten, and names of those schools aren't included on this bronze coin.

I had it made into a beautiful necklace and Louise wears it to Iowa sporting activities and special events. Iowa fans are always interested in her necklace and stop to admire it and ask her questions. I have no idea of its monetary worth, but it's priceless to Louise and me.

Bill Quinby

Sports Opinion

I started a television talk show about Iowa sports in 1985. It was called Sports Opinion. We recorded the show on public access television, PATV. My son Joe took care of all of the video recording production. I used to line up the guests and decide what our topics would be, and then Dirk Keller took over the role as host. Most recently, other panel members have been Bob Boyd, Bud Sueppel, and Pat White. Other panel members have included John Murphy, Al Grady, John Balmer, and Tom Brandt. We interviewed coaches, athletes, and athletic directors on the show. We primarily discussed local high school and Hawkeye men's and women's sports.

Bob Boyd, Dirk Keller, special guest Iowa Athletic Director Gary Barta, Earle Murphy and Bud Sueppel are pictured on stage during a filming of Sports Opinion.
At the end of the show, Dirk Keller always signed off with: *"Either you're a Hawk, or you're Not!"*

The show was first recorded in the public library. John Hess asked me to host a local sports show. At first I was pretty nervous, but quickly realized how much fun it was. I enjoyed filming the show each Wednesday. Due to PATV budget issues and scheduling conflicts, after 30 years, our last weekly show was filmed in December 2015.

We have had fun after the show too.
Dirk & Iowa Keller, Louise & Murph, Judy & Bob Boyd

We have even filmed in my back yard.
John Murphy, John Balmer, Al Grady, Murph

Murph Remembers...

Earle Murphy's Response in *The Rotary Round Up* Iowa City Rotary Club

September 3, 1987
The following is a response to the message of last week's speaker at Rotary who was critical of the University of Iowa Children's Hospital system:

I'm not handicapped---I'm crippled!!
I had Polio when I was 6 years old. I would like very much to tell you of **my** experiences at the Children's Hospital.

My first operation on my foot was when I was 11 years old--- the last when I was 25.

Every medical procedure that was preformed on me was absolutely free, my early dental care was done during the great depression and I still have all my teeth.

The ward that I was on might not be described as happy time USA, but it wasn't as bad as pictured to this group last week.

Indignities
Oh yes, but you had to ask yourself, "Was it worth it?" "It certainly was!"

I was paraded nude in front of the doctors and nurses and I was embarrassed…we all know the science of walking is quite complicated. During my hospitalizations, Dr. Steindler and his staff took care of me. I benefitted from his knowledge and medical expertise.

Need for Love and Hugs
Sure --- that's a part of human life, and you have to take advantage of what's at hand. At the Children's Hospital, there was a man who came every Sunday and handed out sticks of gum. I got my love from the caring of the Gum Man.

My doctors called me "Spud" and gave me an occasional squeeze on my shoulder.

Sometimes the nurses allowed me to 'help' on the wards, and that made me feel special.

When my mom came to visit me, she always ended her visit with a hug.

I would like to make one final remark.
I was 25 years old when I had my last operation at Children's Hospital.
I graduated with honors!
That operation was a rip-roaring success. And for that I will be eternally grateful.

That message was from about as deep in the 'heart' as one can go. Now you know why I think Murph is one of the world's tallest leprechauns---he's enchanted and enchanting!   Ken Dolan, Rotary Round Up Editor

The 1987 Holiday Bowl *"I can only do it once"*

Louise and I were in San Diego for the 1987 Holiday Bowl. Iowa had just completed a 10-3 season. We were just heading to our seats at the Jack Murphy stadium when Earl Yoder sees us and yells down, "Murph, stay put! Shirley Fry has been looking for you and wants you to join her." Wow, that's great.

Shirley did find us, and as a result, Louise and I join Shirley and Ann Brashier in their fantastic press box seats. The best seats in the house!

As the game against Wyoming unfolds Iowa isn't doing too well. And, losing isn't any fun. The coach's wives are really anxious. Iowa's down 19-7 in the fourth quarter.

Shirley looks at me and demands "Do something Murph!" I say, "Okay…here's what's gonna happen. Their quarterback is going throw the ball and then we are going to intercept it and go for a touchdown." And she says, "Really?" I say, 'Yes Really."

So, on the very next play, the Wyoming quarterback goes back for a pass, throws the ball and Anthony Wright our cornerback intercepts the pass and runs 33 yards for a touchdown.

The girls are going crazy! Shirley is hugging me. Ann's got her arms around me, hugging me too. Louise can't believe it and neither can I! The score is now 19-14, and we have new hope for our Hawkeyes.

Still excited, Shirley asks, "Murph, what are you going to do next?" I reply, "Nothing, I can only do that once a game!"

Iowa went on to score another TD and won the bowl game 20-19.

October 1988 Road Trip

The next fall I am driving the girls to the Iowa-Indiana football game. Shirley Fry and Ann Brashier are in the back seat and Louise is up front with me. I'm driving along I-80 just a few miles from Davenport, at about 9:00 Friday morning, when I notice red lights flashing in my rearview mirror. I glance at the speedometer and I'm going 75 mph. As the patrol officer approaches the car I realize I know him. He says "Hi Murph how are you?" I ask him if there's any way he can give me a break. He tells me there's no way and he points up at the sky. Oh, the highway patrol airplane has spotted me… so I got the ticket.

Jimmy Rodgers and the 1991 Rose Bowl

I first met Jimmy Rodgers when he played basketball for the University of Iowa. He was an excellent guard and voted team MVP in 1963-64 and 1964-65. One of my best memories of his playing days was when Iowa beat UCLA on January 29th, 1965. Our Ralph Miller coached team beat the #1 ranked John Wooden coached team 87-82. UCLA dominated college basketball during that era, winning 10 NCAA national championships between 1964 and 1975.

Jimmy's long career coaching basketball took him to the highest level. He was an assistant coach for years on teams that won six NBA championships. He coached two of the all-time greats in Larry Bird and Michael Jordan. He was the head coach of the Boston Celtics for two years, but was fired in May 1990 with three years left on his contract. That gave him some time to take a year off and enjoy watching his son play college football for the Iowa Hawkeyes.

Jimmy's son is Matt Rodgers, who quarterbacked Iowa in the 1991 Rose Bowl. Jimmy was able to enjoy the 1990 football season and his son's success. Matt was named the Big Ten football offensive MVP in 1990. He was also named first team All-Big Ten quarterback for the 1990 and 1991 seasons.

Louise and I were in Pasadena for the 1991 Rose Bowl, Our friends Chuck and Patricia Frandson lived in Sherman Oaks, California. They were very involved volunteers and supporters of the Rose Bowl parade and festivities. The day before the game, they invited us to join them to tour the Rose Bowl stadium. We were down on the football field and I saw Jimmy Rodgers. We visited for a while and I asked him if he and his wife had plans for the evening. The Frandsons were hosting a dinner party and had told us we could invite another couple. The Rodger's accepted and joined us for a wonderful evening. We laughed as Mrs. Rodgers joked about how different it was having Jimmy around the house all the time. He would ask her what they were going to do tomorrow…and she'd smile and say, "You're on your own. I'm going to lunch with the girls."

Jimmy Rodgers and Matt Rodgers were both great Hawkeyes. There have been several examples of sons following their fathers to Iowa and having successful athletic careers.

What makes this more unique is that Jimmy played basketball and Matt played football.

Garden Club

I often had lunch with Bump Elliott and Doug Goodfellow downtown at the Holiday Inn. One day I told Bump I thought we should have lunch on a regular basis and see if we could find some more friends who would like to come and eat with us. Bump immediately liked the idea and said he had two suggestions. "Let's call it 'Garden Club' and, Murph; you will be the "President for Life". That was back in the late 1980's and Garden Club is still going strong to this day.

The idea behind the Garden Club name was because the restaurant where we were eating was decorated with lots of flowers and hanging vines, and it really felt like being in a garden. We invited Francis Cretzmeyer and Doug Goodfellow as original members. Our original Garden Club had four members.

Our first year we grew to about 20 members and our lunch meetings were held in a reserved room at the Holiday Inn Downtown. We would sometimes invite guests, to come and join us. After a few years we had grown to about 50 members and moved across town to the University Athletic Club. The meetings became something to really look forward to. And as members talked to their friends, more people wanted IN! I always approved every applicant, as the President for Life. One day we realized that we'd outgrown the amenities of the UAC and Bob Bowlsby suggested that the lunch meetings could be held in the University of Iowa Athletic Hall of Fame Museum. I was surprised and asked, "Could we really do that?" He looked at me very thoughtfully and replied, "Since I am the University of Iowa Athletic Director, I can probably make it happen." We have been meeting in this spot, at the U I Hall of Fame building since 2004 and we often fill up the room with 65 members.

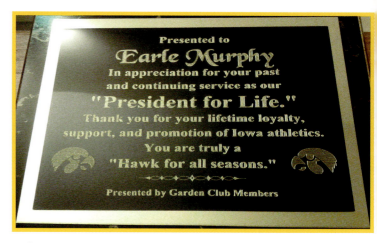

Our 'Men Only' group meets the Friday before every home football game from 11:15 to 1:00. The program includes lunch, Iowa cheers, singing, jokes, and a few speakers. Darrell Wyrick was our head cheerleader and joke teller for years, and did a fantastic job. Bill Olin is our song leader, Mike Gatens leads some cheers, and Jim Conard challenges us with Hawkeye trivia contests.

I was the master of ceremonies until 2012 when I retired and my son, John Murphy, took over at the helm. The men who attend our meetings range in ages from 40 to 92 years old. All are enthusiastic Hawkeye supporters who look forward to having fun, dancing the Hokey Pokey, singing songs, doing the I-O-W-A locomotive cheer and loving their Hawks. I might have retired my role as the meeting organizer, but I am still the "President for Life" and happily attend every meeting.

Garden Club program fun with Darrell Wyrick

Photo Courtesy of Mark Wilson

Decade Seven | 1983-1992 | 105

Photo courtesy of Bob Goodfellow

Head Coaches: Forest Evashevski, Jerry Burns, Hayden Fry, and Kirk Ferentz

L-R Hayden Fry, Mike Crawford, Bill Brashier, and George Wine.

Mike Crawford explains the history of the Grantland Rice Trophy

Past notable Garden Club events

In November of 2006, the Garden Club hosted a reunion celebration of the Rose Bowl football teams. The Hall of Fame Building was packed with former athletes and coaches. It was really amazing to see Forest Evashevski, Jerry Burns, Hayden Fry, and Kirk Ferentz come together to honor past Hawkeye teams.

In 2010, the Garden Club hosted a luncheon for the Iowa Varsity Club. Football players from the Evashevski Era enjoyed their time reminiscing and sharing their experiences with Iowa fans. Garden Club member Mike Crawford helped organize the event.

Our featured speaker the last several years has been former Hawkeye great and NFL tight end Marv Cook. He does a great job giving us his insight on the Hawkeye football team and the upcoming opponent. Marv is currently the head coach at Regina High School. His teams have won a record six consecutive state championships, which included a record 56 game winning streak. We often have an Iowa coach or administrator speak as well.

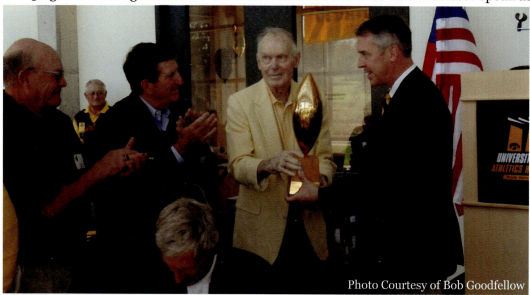

Photo Courtesy of Bob Goodfellow

L to R: Hugh Drake, Randy Duncan, Forest Evashevski, Gary Barta, and Jerry Burns (sitting)

Photo Courtesy of Mark Wilson

Three Athletic Directors at Garden Club
Bob Bowlsby, Bump Elliott, Gary Barta

Marv Cook provides his football expertise each meeting

The National Iowa Varsity Club

340 Carver Hawkeye Arena, #1 Elliott Drive, Iowa City, Iowa 52242-1020, (319) 335-9438, FAX (319) 335-9333
www.iowavarsityclub.com

2010 Board of Directors

P. Sue Beckwith
Waukee, Iowa
Basketball, 1977, 78, 79, 80
Past-President

Trevor R. Bollers
North Liberty, Iowa
Football, 1994, 96, 97, 98

J. Barron Bremner
Iowa City, Iowa
Wrestling, 1957, 58

Michelle C. Conlon
Iowa City, Iowa
Tennis, 1984, 85, 86, 87

Timothy F. Doherty
Iowa City, Iowa
Golf, 1978, 79, 80, 81

Molly C. Gable
Iowa City, Iowa
Swimming, 2002, 03, 04, 05

Matthew J. Hughes
North Liberty, Iowa
Football, 1995, 96, 97, 98

Michael Lavery
Quincy, Illinois
Football, 1966, 67

Lynn R. Tauke Mawe
innell, Iowa
olf, 1983, 84, 85, 86

James G. Milani
Centerville, Iowa
Football, 1952
Track, 1952

Jodi Lynn Parsons
Indianola, Iowa
Track 1991, 92, 93, 94

Robert A. Stein, Sr.
Iowa City, Iowa
Swimming, 1953, 54, 55

Orville H. Townsend
Iowa City, Iowa
Fencing, 1964, 65, 66
Football, 1965
President

David L. Triplett
Iowa City, Iowa
Football, 1970, 71

Paul J. Usinowicz
Powell, Ohio
Football, 1965, 66, 67

Les Steenlage
Coralville, Iowa
Wrestling, 1974
Executive Director

September 14, 2010

Earle Murphy
1692 Ridge Road
Iowa City, IA 52245

Dear Earle,

On behalf of the National Iowa Varsity Club and the Iowa Athletic Department, I would like to thank you for your assistance during the 2010 Varsity Club Weekend.

Thank you for opening the Garden Club Luncheon to the 1960 and Evashevski Era football reunions and their spouses. This was a wonderful gesture on behalf of the Garden Club. Everyone very much enjoyed the experience.

The Varsity Club Weekend is a special event for our award winners, their friends and families, and all Varsity Club members. Everyone had a great time and we appreciate your assistance in making this Varsity Club Weekend such a great success.

Go Hawkeyes!

Sincerely,

Les Steenlage
Executive Director

One of our special Garden Club luncheons was on March 26, 2009, when Barron Bremner discussed the famed Iowa Mau Mau Squad.

Iowa's Mau Mau Squad

QB	Olin Treadway
QB	Ron Bosrock
T	Barron Bremner
T	Ernie Mielke
G	Dominic Sgro
C	John Leshyn
E	Dick Livermore
E	Ray Stagich
FB	Jon Jonda
HB	Mel Knotts
HB	Jack McDonald

THE IOWA MAU MAU TEAM

"Something of Value", a movie based on a novel by Robert Ruark was the inspiration for the well-known Iowa Hawkeye "Mau Maus" during the championship Rose Bowl years of Forest Evashevski in the 1950's. Hawkeye sophomores Barron Bremner and Ernie Mielke, accompanied by several other football players, attended the movie at the old Englert Theatre. Walking to their dormitory after the Sunday evening movie, the players discussed their admiration for the courage, skills, and ferocity of the Mau Mau warriors in their fight for independence.

Bremner approached members of the coaching staff the next day, suggesting that he could put together eleven members of the football team who saw little action on Saturdays, who were themselves warriors not unlike the Mau Mau freedom fighters, and were a valuable, underused resource to the team.

The staff gave approval for Bremner to form a team for mid-week scrimmages against the starting team. Inasmuch as a very limited NCAA substitution rule was in effect at that time, very few men played on game day. Players were required to play both offense and defense. On defense, the center and fullback played linebacker, the quarterback played safety, and linemen and halfbacks played the same relative positions as on offense. There were no kicking teams, return teams, field-goal teams, or designated offensive or defensive teams. This new Mau Mau team would give eleven men an opportunity for game-type action on Tuesdays and Wednesdays, and would give the starting team a more game-like situation in preparing for the next Saturday's opponent than currently existed with a member of the coaching staff holding up cardboard diagrams of plays.

Bremner was the organizer and captain of the Mau Muas and was responsible for selecting the team members, overseeing preparation to present game-like situations for the starting team by running the upcoming opponents' offensive and defensive schemes. Toughness and attitude were primary requisites in Bremner's selection of team members. His first selection to join him on the Mau Mau team was fellow sophomore tackle, Ernie Mielke, who Bremner said was pound-for pound as tough and ornery as any man on the football team. Others selected were ends Ray Stagich and Dick Livermore, guards Dominic Sgro and Don Shipanie, center John Leshyn, quarterback Ron Bosrock, fullback Jon Janda, with Mel Knotts and Jack McDonald at halfback. Other players were occasionally drafted from a waiting list to join the Mau Maus, but this eleven-man lineup would change only in the event of a season-ending injury creating a team opening. "Owwies" were not considered a reason for lineup changes.

"They consider themselves an independent team — a rival of the varsity. When they scrimmage the play is rough and rugged.", said columnist Bill McGrane of the Des Moines Tribune. *"Archie Kodros sometimes serves as the Mau Mau coach, but the actual leader, captain, and manager is Barron Bremner, a 212 pound tackle from Iowa Falls."*

I always ask Kirk the same thing: "Can I call the first play?" And he always says, "No."

The Hawk, the Street and the Scholarship

I had a three-step plan to honor my friend Bump Elliott upon his retirement as the University of Iowa's athletic director. I wanted to get the name of the street Woolf Avenue changed to Elliott Drive. I wanted to establish a $100,000 scholarship in Bump's name for Iowa football players. And, I wanted to get a sculpture of the hawk that was in a farm field north of town moved to a future park across from Carver-Hawkeye Arena.

I had the ideas... I just had no idea what it would take to get it all accomplished.

In June 1989, Louise and I met with Barb and Bump at their home. Outside there was a full moon and lightning; inside we sipped iced tea. Bump said, "What's happening?" I replied, "People have been coming into Bremers and asking "What can we do for Bump when he retires?" Since I agree with them that something should be done for you, I have come up with three ideas. I then explained them to Bump and Barb.

Bump asked, "Who would be on the committee?"
I said, "Just me and I report to you!"
Bump said, "That's fine."
Barb said, "I think we need the Hawk."

Here's what happened during the months that followed...from that first conversation at Bump's to the ribbon cutting ceremony on November 10, 1990 when we dedicated the "Hawk" to Bump.

The easiest of the three was getting the street name changed. I met with the Iowa City planning committee and explained the plan. The University of Iowa's Campus Planning Committee and the State Board of Regents endorsed the street name change. Once the change from Woolf Avenue to Elliott Drive was approved, two signs were made. One sign was spelled incorrectly as: Elliot Drive. But, the other sign was made correctly: Elliott Drive. That fall, prior to the start of the Iowa football season, the street signs were in place. I had accomplished my first goal in less than three months!

I proposed the idea of creating the scholarship for Bump to the UI Foundation. They mailed out letters, made phone calls, and raised the money. Our goal to endow the C.W. "Bump" Elliott Scholarship was quickly accomplished.

The final step, getting the "Hawk" was a challenge. Dave Lawton, who was an art student at the University of Iowa, had sculpted "Strike Force," or what we call

left: Dave Lawton, the creator and sculptor of "The Hawk"

top: Louise jumps on the pedestal

left: Setting the Hawk in place

the "Hawk". The statue is 13 feet tall and 1,500 pounds of stainless steel. He had recently left Iowa and moved to Chico, California.

I was aware that several attempts had been made to purchase the sculpture by past coaches and members of the U of I athletic departments, but no one had had any success convincing Dave to sell the Hawk. I contacted Dave by phone and he was receptive and liked our idea and where the sculpture would be located. Larry Bruner, associate athletic director of finance was also working to obtain the money to buy the Hawk.

As though getting the Hawk wasn't hard enough, the Campus Planning Committee didn't like the Hawk, and felt it wasn't a proper art display for the university. When I heard that I said, "If the university didn't want it I could get it displayed in downtown Iowa City!" I knew members of the Iowa City Council would love it on the corner of Clinton Street and Iowa Avenue. This pressured the committee to make a decision. Joyce Summerwill, a member of the committee, agreed with me that the Hawk was a fitting tribute to Bump and should be approved by the planning committee. The last meeting I had with the committee was in late July. I remember getting a phone call that we would be meeting at 10 o'clock the next morning. I knew I had to be at the meeting, but I had promised my daughter Ann and her children that we would go to Minneapolis early that morning to attend a Minnesota Twins-Oakland A's baseball game that night. Delaying our trip would mean the game was off. When I explained that I had to stay for the meeting, they agreed, knowing how much time and energy had already gone into this project. Well, it's a good thing I went! It was at this meeting that I convinced the group to endorse the plan to bring the Hawk sculpture to campus.

Even with the delay, I was still able to take Louise, Ann and our two grandchildren to the baseball game. I really think if I hadn't gone to the meeting...the Hawk project would have failed.

We were having Bump's retirement party at the UI Memorial Union Ballroom. My son, Joe Murphy, who owns Murphy Sound, had set up the music, lights, and projectors for the event. I had planned to unveil "Bump's Gifts" to the Iowa fans in attendance. The street signs for Elliott Drive were ready and models were on display. The $100,000 Athletic Scholarship was well in the works. The one-acre plot of land to house "The Hawk" was just south of Carver Arena had been acquired. And it looked like we were finally getting the Hawk.

I got a phone call from Larry Bruner late that afternoon. We both thought getting the Hawk was a done deal, but suddenly there was a last minute snag. Dave wanted $5,000 more than had been offered. Larry told me not to mention the Hawk at the party. I went home and told Louise that I couldn't mention the Hawk. I was so disappointed, and I just couldn't let it rest. So I called Dave and thank god he answered his phone.

left: Louise and Murph with the Hawk

below: Murph and Bump at the dedication

IOWA

DEPARTMENT OF INTERCOLLEGIATE ATHLETICS

C. W. (BUMP) ELLIOTT
Director of Athletics

11/14/90

Dear Murph,

Allow me a moment to, again, thank you for your personal efforts, as a friend, in making it a reality that the "Hawk" has indeed arrived. I know many people contributed to this project but it has been your determination that has made this possible. Most of all, your insistence that it honor me has been one of the most meaningful honors of my life. The ceremony last Saturday was really perfect and I deeply appreciate your kind words "My friend, Bump". I can only respond in saying "My great and dear friend Louise and Earl Murphy" made this all possible.

Hawkeye fans for years to come will have the joy seeing the "Hawk" and know a true Hawkeye, Earl Murphy, made it all possible.

Your friend,
Bump

I told him that I had just heard that he wanted another five grand for the Hawk. He said that was what he wanted. So, I told him about a conversation I had overheard when I was trying to get permission for the Hawk to come to campus.

One of your former art professors had said,

"Over my dead body, will that sculpture ever come to Iowa City!"

So, I said to Dave, "Let's bury that old professor." He agreed and said, "Let's do it!"

There was no more discussion of the additional $5,000.

I arrived at the Memorial Union for Bump's party and immediately saw Larry Bruner across the room. I excitedly gave him my best fist pump and he just hit his forehead in relief knowing I had succeeded in landing the Hawk!

I looked at Joe and gave him a 'thumbs up'. He knew just what to do. His slide show began and when the picture of Strike Force, the Hawk, was displayed the crowd cheered. After the show ended, Shirley Fry came up behind where I was sitting and put her hands on my shoulders. She wanted to know how I had done it. I just smiled at her and said, "There's always a way."

The day the Hawk came to Iowa City was really exciting. The park had been cleared and the site where the sculpture would rest was ready. The architects had done a great job. The crane was there to set it in its place. The concrete pedestal was already in place and Louise spontaneously jumped up on it and gave a cheer. Louise and I were so happy. So much had taken place, so much time had been spent, and so much energy had gone into this moment. And finally, the Hawk was where it should be.

On November 10, 1990 before the Iowa - Ohio State football game Strike Force, our Hawk, was dedicated to Bump. I was the emcee at the ceremony. I explained that the Hawk sculpture, in addition to honoring Bump, is meant to symbolize all past, present and future athletes and fans of the University of Iowa sports programs.

Afterwards Bump told me that, "This was one of the happiest days of my life."

The Plaque for Strike Force

The Hawk
November 10, 1990

"Presented to the University of Iowa in honor of C.W. "Bump" Elliott.

Chalmers W. Elliott- "Bump" to his many friends and fans- guided the University of Iowa men's intercollegiate athletic program to a position of national respect and prominence during his tenure as director of men's athletics. Under Elliott, the decade of the 1980's was one of the most successful in the University of Iowa athletic history, marked by numerous bowl games, championships, and NCAA post-season tournament appearances.

Elliott is the only person to appear in the Rose Bowl in five different capacities: student athlete, assistant coach, head coach, assistant athletic director and athletic director. He was named director of men's athletics at the University of Iowa in 1970, following 13 years as coach and administrator at his alma mater, the University of Michigan. Those years were highlighted by a Big Ten title and Rose Bowl victory. In 1989 Elliott was inducted into the National College Football Hall of Fame and the Rose Bowl Hall of Fame.

A native of Bloomington, Illinois, Elliott played three sports as a student-athlete at Michigan from 1946 to 1948. An All-American halfback, he was the Big Ten's leading scorer and most valuable player in 1947. He also played portions of the 1943 and 1944 football seasons at Purdue University.

Bump and his wife, Barbara, have two sons, Bill and Bob and a daughter, Betsy.

The Hawk was created from stainless steel by sculpture David Lawton of Chico, California, formerly of Iowa City.

The plaque was designed by architects Hansen Lind Meyer Inc. Iowa City."

Typed copy of letter from John Streif
UI Athletic Trainer

Thanks so very much for initiating and following through on the very beautiful Elliott Park. It couldn't be a more fitting tribute to such an outstanding person and what he has done for this great University. It is such a perfect display for our athletic facilities as well as the entrance to campus. Thanks for all you have done on this very special as well as your continued support and enthusiasm.

John Streif

Joe Murphy Remembers...

I worked at Bremers during the time Dad was trying to bring Strike Force to the Iowa Campus. These are some of my memories.

In order to decide the best place on campus to display the sculpture, Dad devised a plan. He wanted to find the best setting, where the Hawk would be enhanced by natural light. He had me make up a pole contraption that was the exact height of the Hawk. It was comprised of a couple of 2"x4"s that I could easily take apart and bolt together; this way it would fit in my truck and I could check out locations. Dad wanted to get a feeling of the height and spacing that Strike Force would need to be most visible. It must have seemed odd to watch me assemble the pole and just watch it... little did people know I was on a mission to find the perfect area for the Hawk! We visited five to six places on campus: near Old Capitol, Kinnick Stadium, the old tennis courts and other locations. Dad finally picked out a spot that would be in sight as you drove along Hawkins Drive. The best part was it was a narrow strip of land between a parking lot and the outfield fence of the baseball diamond. This particular area was not well maintained and seemed readily available. It was also a central location for many Iowa athletic activities.

The amount of work Dad did to get the Hawk on campus was intense and interesting. There were at least six meetings that I knew about and one that I got to sit in on. An Arts on Campus committee of four or five university employees were in the Bremers office; one of whom was a highly regarded artist and professor. I heard these words spew out of his mouth regarding the Hawk: *Over my dead body will the Hawk ever be brought onto University property and that is final!*

Earle had sat patiently, letting them run the meeting. At that point, Dad said "No problem, it will not go on U of I property. It will be placed at the intersection of Iowa Avenue and Clinton Street. We will use about six parking spaces and build a site for the Hawk." I really did not understand what was going on but I realized he had called them on their words. If the Hawk went up at that location, EVERY picture taken of the Old Capitol from the east side of Iowa Avenue would include the Hawk and a salute to Bump and Hawkeye Athletics. The response from the committee was: "The City will Never allow this." The response from Earle was to inform the group that if this was an unacceptable location, they should approve the site he wanted on Hawkins Drive.

And, Earle wasn't finished. He said that no matter what their decision was, the street in front of Carver Hawkeye Arena was being renamed Elliott Drive, in honor of Bump Elliott. Once again they were not happy about another of his ideas. The committee felt there was no way the city would allow the street to be renamed.

At that point, Dad told me to reach under his desk and to pull out a newly made Iowa City street sign. Dad told them the street name change was already approved and done. I stood there proudly holding the Elliott Drive sign. The committee then realized they had been beaten and agreed to placing Strike Force behind the baseball diamond. I think Dad would have been a pretty good chess player.

In September 2012, after an Iowa football game, my daughter, Ann took me to see the Hawk. I think the Hawk and I still look good after 22 years.

I spent time remembering all of my efforts to get it in place and visiting with people as they came by to admire the sculpture.

The following are excerpts from a letter written to Murph and Louise by Dave Lawton, the creator and sculptor of "The Hawk".

"Thank you for your great efforts and sacrifice of personal time in making the "Hawk Project" a first rate achievement. If it wasn't for your dedication to the project, plus a desire to see it on the Iowa campus, it would still be on a farm north of Coralville."

The "Hawk" Sculpture and Elliott Park Contributors

There were several people and businesses that donated their time and services to make the Hawk sculpture project more affordable for the University of Iowa. They all enjoyed being involved in a project that honored Bump Elliott.

Thanks to Bump for allowing the project to happen, and thanks to Dave Lawton for selling the sculpture at a very fair price. The chart on this page tracked the progress and timing of the jobs needed to complete the project. Architects John Lind, Larry Morgan and Ed Michelson from Hansen Lind Meyer designed the park, and Hugh Jennings was the site manager.

Special thanks to Tom Werderitsch, Max Selzer, Earl Yoder, Bob Thompson, Dennis Dykstra, John Moreland, Ken Gerard, Bob Barker, Jeff Maxwell, Dave Streb, Bob Wolf, Ted Thorn, Bill Condon, Bob Edwards, Larry Millman, and Phil Oldis.

Besides the huge job of transporting and setting "The Hawk" sculpture into place, they contributed by providing grading, landscaping, sidewalks, brick pavers, trees, sod, etc.

Thanks to all involved!

IN MEMORY OF
CHRIS STREET

CHRIS STREET, A 6'-8" JUNIOR FORWARD FOR THE HAWKEYES, WAS KILLED IN AN AUTO ACCIDENT IN IOWA CITY JANUARY 19, 1993, TWO WEEKS PRIOR TO HIS 21ST BIRTHDAY, ONE MONTH AFTER BEING NAMED MVP OF THE 1992 SAN JUAN SHOOTOUT, AND JUST THREE DAYS AFTER SETTING AN IOWA RECORD OF 34 STRAIGHT FREE THROWS.

A THREE SPORT HIGH SCHOOL STANDOUT FROM INDIANOLA, IOWA, CHRIS EARNED A SPECIAL PLACE IN THE HEARTS OF IOWA FANS WITH HIS HUSTLE, HARD WORK, AND ENTHUSIASM.

"CHRIS STREET REPRESENTED ALL THAT IS GOOD ABOUT THE MIDWEST AND THE STATE OF IOWA," SAID IOWA BASKETBALL COACH TOM DAVIS. "HE WAS OPEN, CARING, HONEST, LOVING, AND LIVED LIFE TO THE FULLEST EVERY DAY. HE WAS ONE OF THE GREATEST HAWKEYES OF ALL TIME."

JOHNSON COUNTY I-CLUB
NOVEMBER 6, 1993

It was appropriate that a memorial tribute to honor Chris Street was placed in Elliott Park, across the street from Carver-Hawkeye arena.

The Floyd of Rosedale Trophy

The trophy is contested for every year during the Iowa-Minnesota football game. The trophy is usually on display at the U of I football complex. But sometimes it travels to Bremers, where lots of Hawkeye fans can admire it and actually touch it. On November 23, 1991 the Floyd of Rosedale trophy even made a hospital call. I had a serious stroke when I was 68 years old and was hospitalized at Mercy Hospital. I was still in the hospital on "Game Day" when Iowa's football operations employees delivered the trophy to my hospital room after Iowa beat Minnesota by a score of 23-8. Nurses and doctors alike could not believe that the real Floyd of Rosedale trophy was in Mercy Hospital.

It was a very kind gesture by the football program and I really appreciated it.

Floyd stayed in my room for a few days and then was taken to Bremers.

Murph with grandchildren Bill and Kate Pearson, and the Floyd of Rosedale Trophy

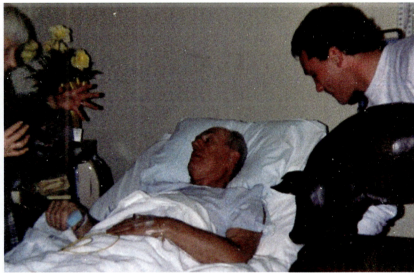

On the far left Louise is so excited! She is telling me that Floyd is in my hospital room. Jerry Murphy is next to Floyd.

Smiling with Floyd, we are both happy to be back at Bremers!

Reunited with Floyd of Rosedale in 2015

Bob Downer
Iowa City
Community Leader and Board of Regent

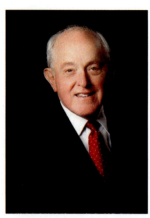

Bob Downer has been my attorney and friend for a long time. Bob is a partner with Meardon, Sueppel & Downer in Iowa City, where he's practiced law for 53 years. He attended the University of Iowa and was Student Body President in 1960. He's been a community leader in Iowa City and the State of Iowa ever since.

Bob served as President of the Iowa City Chamber of Commerce, and President of the Iowa City Noon Rotary Club. He's also served on numerous other boards, including leadership roles with the Iowa City Public Library and Iowa City Area Development (ICAD). The UI College of Law honored Bob as recipient of the Alumni Achievement Award in 2013.

Bob always expressed interest in serving on the state Board of Regents. In 2003, he was surprised and honored when Governor Tom Vilsack told him of his plans to make him a regent. Bob says about the appointment, "I still find irony in the fact that the first non-student representative from Johnson County to the Board of Regents was a Republican," He served two six-year terms, from 2003 to 2015, and advocated for the funding of new building projects on the three state campuses.

Bob's had Iowa basketball season tickets for 51 years, and football season tickets for 48. We're lucky to have people like Bob Downer working and volunteering in our community.

Bump Elliott and Wayne Duke

Bump Elliott, presenting a chair and plaque to his good friend and retiring Big Ten Commissioner Wayne Duke at Kinnick Stadium in 1989. A native of Burlington, Iowa, Duke graduated from Iowa in 1950 and was the Big Ten Commissioner from 1971-1989.

Murph Remembers...

Decade Eight | 1993-2002

"Murph remembers..."

My University of Iowa "Mount Rushmore"

It's been an honor to have lived in Iowa City and to have known so many amazing people who have worked at the University of Iowa.

Here are the four employees who I think have made the most positive impact on the University of Iowa in the last 50 years.

Willard "Sandy" Boyd

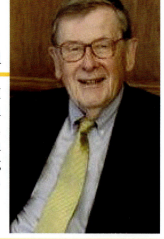

Willard "Sandy" Boyd was the President of the UI from 1969-1981. He led the school during the Vietnam protest years and grew enrollment during his tenure. Sandy was a law professor for numerous years at Iowa before and after being President. The Boyd Law Building on campus is named for him.

John Colloton

John Colloton was the Director and CEO of the UI Hospitals & Clinics from 1971-1993.

Under his leadership the hospital grew into a world renowned teaching hospital, and employs more than 7,000 people.

Darrell Wyrick

Darrell Wyrick was the first full time employee and President of the UI Foundation from 1962-1998. Under his leadership, the UI Foundation grew to more Than one hundred employees who raised more than $500 million for the University of Iowa.

Chalmers "Bump" Elliott

Bump was the UI Athletic Director from 1970-1991. He led the athletic department to unprecedented growth and success. He hired great coaches, including Hayden Fry, Dan Gable, Lute Olson, and Dr. Tom Davis.

Statue in downtown Iowa City, corner of Linn St and Iowa Ave
Irving B. Weber
1900-1997
Historian, Humanitarian, All-American Swimmer, Businessman, Gentleman

Town Historian Irving Weber and Earle Murphy

Al Grady, Earle Murphy, and George Wine enjoying conversation and laughs in the office at Bremers.

Dan Gable is the best athlete and coach of any sport…ever.

Dan Gable is one of a kind. His intensity and work ethic is legendary. His success as a wrestler and coach is unmatched.

Dan's overall record in high school and college was 181–1. He won a Gold Medal at the 1972 Olympic Games held in Munich, Germany. In 1999, Sports Illustrated selected Dan Gable as the greatest sports figure in the history of the state of Iowa. He was also named the top wrestler of the 20th Century by Gannett News Service.

He was hired as the head wrestling coach at Iowa in 1976, and initially Dan was quiet and shy. The first several times he spoke at Johnson County I-Club events, he was not a very good public speaker. But, in typical Gable fashion, he worked hard at it and Dan became an excellent speaker.

I'm the proud owner of a print by famous artist LeRoy Neiman, featuring Dan Gable. It's called Gable's Gold, and it's one of my favorite pieces of art.

In 1986, Iowa City was host to the NCAA wrestling championships. The University of Iowa had not hosted the tournament since 1959, so it was exciting to have the best teams and wrestlers in Iowa City. I asked Kathy Gable, Dan's wife, if we could have any of Dan's memorabilia for a front window display at Bremers. She agreed, and on the week of the event she brought several items to the store, including Dan's Olympic Gold medal. Wrestling fans from all over the country were able to see the gold medal. It was very nice of Dan and Kathy to share it with everyone.

Dan Gable led the Iowa wrestling program to 15 NCAA team titles, and 21 consecutive Big Ten titles. He coached 45 National Champions and 106 Big Ten Champions. His career coaching record was 355-21-5.

John Wooden is often thought to be the greatest coach in the history of sport. Let's compare his coaching record with Gable's. Wooden won 80% of all the basketball games he coached. Gable won 93% of all of the wrestling meets he coached.

Gable wins again!

Photo courtesy of UI Athletics Department

Decade Eight | 1993-2002 121

Photo courtesy of UI Athletics Department

Tim Dwight
Superman wears #6 and he plays for the Iowa Hawkeyes

I think Tim Dwight is the most exciting punt returner ever to wear an Iowa uniform. His quickness and speed also made him a great wide receiver. As a record setting athlete at City High in Iowa City, I had the opportunity to closely follow his entire career.

As a 15 year-old City High freshman, Tim was called up to play in a varsity playoff game. He sprinted 80 yards for a touchdown the first time he touched the ball. A local legend was born that day. During his high school career, Tim rushed for 4,148 yards, scored 81 touchdowns, and had 11 interceptions. Tim was named the Iowa High School Player of the Year, and named to the Parade High School All-American team.

Tim Dwight was also a legendary track and field athlete. At City High, he won a record 12 state track titles (eight individuals and four relays), winning the 200 meter dash four times and the long jump three times. He set all-time records in the indoor 400 (:48.73), the 200 (:20.72), and the 100 (:10.19). His high school track coach John Raffensperger says, "Tim Dwight was not only our most talented athlete, but also our hardest worker."

Tim continued his dominance on the track at the University of Iowa; where he was named the MVP of the Big Ten track meet his final semester.

Tim burst on the scene his sophomore year at Iowa as a receiver and punt returner. At 5"9" and 180 pounds, he was often the smallest player on the field, but also the quickest and most explosive. He was such a threat on special teams that opponents would often intentionally kick the ball out of bounds, instead of allowing him to make a long return.

Going into his senior year, some friends and I discussed if there was anything we could do to help promote Tim Dwight for the Heisman Trophy. Steve Droll, Joe Wegman, John Murphy, and I all agreed that Tim embodied many of the right attributes needed to win this prestigious award. The Heisman Trophy is supposed to be awarded to a college football player who best exhibits the pursuit of excellence with integrity. Winners should also epitomize great ability combined with diligence, perseverance, and hard work. We thought that Tim could be a fitting winner of this award, and we set out to assist in any way we could.

We had a few ideas. Of course, this was before the internet, and videos couldn't be posted easily to a large audience. We wanted to produce a local cable TV program featuring Tim, and we also wanted to produce a "highlight video" that we would send to ESPN, etc. to showcase his talents. First, John Murphy discussed the idea with Tim after a track practice, and he agreed to the concept.

We sent Hayden Fry a letter detailing our plans and asking for his approval. Here is a copy of the letter we sent:

12 time state champion in track.

First team all-state on the undefeated 1993 state championship football team

---

March 27, 1997

Hayden Fry
University of Iowa Athletic Dept.
Iowa City, Iowa 52244

Dear Coach Fry:

Congratulations on a GREAT 1996 Hawkeye Football season. Thanks again for attending the Johnson County I-Club Breakfasts. Hawk fans really enjoy hearing you on this personal level. You have spoken at 106 breakfasts, and your record during that time is 69-34-3.

We are writing to ask for your input, advice and approval of a "concept", concerning Tim Dwight. We have plans to produce a local cable television program featuring Tim. The proposed half-hour show would include several interviews with past and current coaches; video highlights of his career in football and track, and interviews with Tim, his parents and friends, detailing his work ethic, attitude and enthusiasm.

Our goal is twofold: 1. To make a cable-program length video that will be enjoyed by Iowa Citians, and 2: To make a 7-8 minute "highlight" video that would be made available for Heisman Trophy voters, sports magazines, ESPN, etc. This video "highlight" of Tim-returning punts, catching passes, blocking and tackling would make those that are not aware...AWARE!! The production costs of the videotapes, and their associated expenses would be borne by a local "Grass Roots" group, and no part of the expenses will be incurred by the U of I Athletic Dept.

If Tim could gain recognition, and be considered as a "Top 5" Heisman candidate going-into the season, "fate may lend a helping hand-you never know what might happen"! We believe the entire country, given the chance, will acclaim Tims and we certainly understand reservations you might have concerning any Heisman "hype" as it relates to the entire Hawkeye team. Please give this matter your sincere consideration. John Murphy will be in contact within the week.

If you have any questions/concerns, please call John at 338-1142, or 339-5462.

Thank you, and GO HAWKS!!

John Murphy Joe Wegman Steve Droll Earle Murphy

cc: Phil Haddy
cc: Rick Klatt
cc: Fred Mims

Coach Fry responded that the marketing and sports information departments had some ideas and to contact them. We were told by Rick Klatt from Sports Marketing that they were mailing out a poster promoting Tim Dwight and Jason DeVries for post season honors.

Our idea for producing videos to promote Tim did not happen as we had hoped. The video production person we were planning on hiring didn't have the time as he had to work on the new Jumbotron being installed at Kinnick Stadium. Regardless, our hearts were in the right place trying to promote a local, home grown athlete for the Heisman Trophy.

Before the season, Tim was named to the Playboy pre-season all-American team. Five games into the 1997 season, the Hawks record was 4-1 and they were ranked 15th in the country. A key game of the season was our next game at Michigan. They were ranked 5th in the country and led by Charles Woodson and Brian Griese. Our high powered offense was led by Matt Sherman, Tavian Banks, and Tim Dwight. With 11 seconds left in the first half, Iowa forced Michigan to punt out of their end zone. They punted directly to Tim, he found a seam and raced to the end zone as time expired, giving the Hawks a 21-7 halftime lead. In the second half, Michigan took the lead and was ahead 28-24 late in the game. With a minute remaining, Iowa drove to the Michigan 26 yard line with a chance for a last second victory. Unfortunately, Matt Sherman threw an interception and we lost the game. I think losing that game was the turning point of the season. Although Tim had an excellent game, his Heisman hopes were diminished with the Hawks suffered another loss. After the game, it was announced that Sherman had broken his thumb on his throwing hand. Without him, Iowa struggled the rest of the year, finishing with a 7-5 record.

The winner of the 1997 Heisman Trophy played in that Iowa vs. Michigan game. The winner was Charles Woodson. The runner-up was Peyton Manning from Tennessee. Tim Dwight finished in a respectable 7th place.

Tim was a consensus first-team All-American kick returner, and Jared DeVries was named the Big Ten Defensive Lineman of the Year. He was drafted in the 4th round of the 1998 NFL draft by the Atlanta Falcons. In the 1999 Super Bowl against the Denver Broncos, he returned a kickoff 94 yards for a touchdown. Tim had a nice professional career spanning 10 years.

In 2007, The Cedar Rapids Gazette sports staff voted Tim Dwight the all-time greatest athlete from the local area, ahead of Kurt Warner and Zach Johnson.

Tim is currently a solar energy businessman and advocate. He's held a youth football camp at City High each summer for the last 15 years. The Tim Dwight Foundation has contributed more than $285,000 to the UI Children's Hospital. Tim's also donated a full set of hurdles and a timer scoreboard to the City High School track program.

As much as Tim Dwight impressed me on the football field, he's been just as impressive off the field with his generosity and community involvement.

My Iowa City Community Heisman Vote goes to………. Tim Dwight.

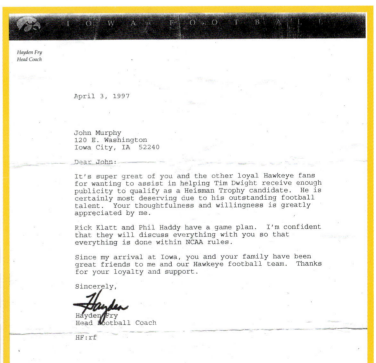

Tailgating with Tim Dwight

"He's got what I call an extra heartbeat. He's the greatest competitor I've had in 46 years of coaching. I can't come up with any new terms because he personifies the great champions in any sport. Pound for pound, heartbeat for heartbeat, he's the competitor of all competitors. His presence energizes the entire team."
Coach Hayden Fry

124 | Murph Remembers...

"To all my friends at Bremers: Thanks for everything! You know your football as well as your clothes! I appreciated all your support." Matt Sherman #12

A Shooting On Campus

My son John, my friend Bump Elliott, and I were on I-80 headed to Columbus, Ohio. It was Friday, November 1, 1991. We were on our way to watch our Iowa Hawkeyes play football at Ohio State. Bump was also planning on spending time visiting some of his relatives while he was there.

We arrived at our hotel room, just about an hour from Columbus at 6 o'clock. The headline story on the nightly news with Peter Jennings was about a mass shooting on the University of Iowa campus. The gunman, 28-year-old Gang Lu, had killed four faculty members and one student before committing suicide. With this tragedy, there was discussion whether the football game should be cancelled.

Bump had just retired as athletic director, so the decision was to be made by the new athletic director, Bob Bowlsby, and President Hunter Rawlings. They decided to play the game and to honor those who were killed. The team removed all markings from their black helmets as a symbolic gesture of mourning. It was a very emotional game for all Iowa fans and players. Iowa played well and posted a rare victory over Ohio State, winning 16-9.

We later learned that Gang Lu was frustrated about not being nominated for an award called the Spriestersbach Prize. He was angry with his professors and the university administration. Lu had also planned on killing President Rawlings, who was saved because he was in Columbus for the Hawkeye football game.

"We had seen enough!" Glenn Vidnovic, John Johnson, and Ken Grabinski

In the early 1990's Bobby Hansen and Mike Gatens helped organize basketball games to raise funds for Iowa farmers. They invited basketball lettermen who ended up playing two games to sellout crowds at Carver-Hawkeye arena. The fans loved seeing all of their favorite former Iowa basketball players.

One of the teams was coached by Glenn Vidnovic and John Johnson. They were both stars on the Ralph Miller coached team that went 14–0 and won the Big Ten championship during the 1970 season. During the first game, the coaches sent their former teammate Ken Grabinski into the game. Ken checked into the game when the first of two free throws was being shot. After the first free throw, and before the second one, the horn sounded. Surprisingly, the coaches sent in a substitute for Ken, as he had only stood on the free throw lane for the one free throw. Ken came off the floor and said "Guys, I was only in the game for one free throw, why are you taking me out now?" Simultaneously, Glenn Vidnovic and John Johnson responded to Ken, "We had seen enough!" I guess, even after 20 years, you can still play great jokes on your teammates!

The benefit alumni games were a huge success and raised over $300,000. Working with Rich Wretman from the UI Foundation, two scholarships were funded with the profits. The first is named "The Iowa Basketball Lettermen's Farm Scholarship." Only children of Iowa farmers are eligible to apply for this freshman year, all tuition paid scholarship. To date, more that 75 students who grew up on an Iowa farm have benefitted from this scholarship. The second endowed scholarship is called "The John Streif Iowa Basketball Lettermen's Scholarship." This scholarship is in honor of John Streif, who served the Iowa basketball, football, and other teams for more than 45 years as an athletic trainer. It funds a scholarship for a student athlete on the Iowa men's basketball team.

One of a Kind

In February of 1993, Ellen Buchanan began producing and hosting a show from the Iowa City Public Library. She had an idea to interview unique people who helped shape the Iowa City community. She came to me because she wanted me to be her first guest. I thought it would be a great program. So we talked and had a wonderful time on *One of a Kind*. She was so pleasant and such a good interviewer.

Trip to Hawaii

I was the grand prizewinner at the Johnson County I-Club party. With one $100 ticket I won the $6,000 prize from the Winebrenner Red Carpet Travel Agency. It was a Hawkeye-Hawaiian cruise for two with Coach Kirk and Mary Ferentz, and his assistant coaches.

After Louise and I landed in Hawaii, we had to take a trolley to board the cruise ship. We were waiting for the trolley with some of the coaches and their wives while a Hawaiian hostess was reading off the names on a list. The people on her list got to board the trolley. All the names were read and she hadn't said, Louise or Earle. That's when we discovered we didn't have shuttle tickets! Kirk says, "I won't go without Murph." The lady tells him that we aren't on the list and can't board. Other people are getting excited too and arguing that we need to get on the trolley. She decides that she'd better make up her mind, and the next thing I hear is, "Okay, you can go." But, I had to buy the tickets, and they were $20 each.

The trolley is crowded but we are having fun. Our vacation is underway.

We had a great bon voyage party as the ship was leaving the dock. The trip was fantastic. It was a great way to vacation in Hawaii, good weather and Hawkeye fans!

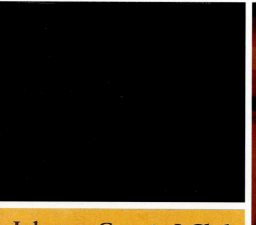
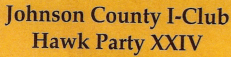

 # Murph Remembers...

Decade Nine | 2003-2012

The Louise and Earle Murphy Athletic Scholarship

This was a surprise. The planning was kept a secret. The results were fantastic!

Beginning in 2008, my son John began talking with his brothers and sisters about endowing a University of Iowa athletic scholarship in our name. They discussed how to go about it, and who would actually do the work. John had the contacts in Iowa City to get the job done. Everyone in the family liked the idea, so the scholarship project was underway.

John and his wife Bonnie worked out the kinks. They enlisted the help of two of our friends, Bump Elliott, and Darrell Wyrick, who supported the idea and agreed to sign the fundraising letter. A mailing list was developed and an informational letter was written. In April of 2009, a packet of information and pledge forms were mailed to numerous friends and relatives. The decision had been made to keep this all a secret... we weren't supposed to find out about it until all of the money was raised and the scholarship was finalized.

But, one summer day, Louise and I received a letter from the University of Iowa Foundation regarding a donation to the scholarship. We were really confused. Did we owe money? Had the foundation made a mistake? What was going on? That evening our son Joe stopped by the house. We asked him about it, and he said to call John. So, we called John and he said he'd be right over.

About an hour later, John and Bonnie arrived. John proceeded to tell us about the scholarship. He showed us the letters and the photos that had been sent out to our family and friends. We were overwhelmed; we were excited, and surprised that all of this had been done without us knowing about it! Now that the secret was out, we could enjoy the process. We were so honored that our names would forever be linked to Iowa athletics.

On a football Saturday, October 10, 2009, a party was held at the Elk's Club to celebrate the pending scholarship and to thank all of the contributors. It was capped off with a victory over Michigan at Kinnick Stadium.

Many of the contributors made yearly donations over a three-year time frame. The Earle and Louise Murphy Athletic Scholarship was fully endowed in 2011. As of the fall of 2013, we have had three scholarship recipients. It was an amazing time. We were honored on the field at halftime of an Iowa home game. We were honored at an Iowa-wrestling match. We have really enjoyed it.

I am really glad that my family decided to honor us with this scholarship now, as I recently discovered the initial thought was about doing it once we were deceased. We would have missed all of the fun!

Our Family

Bump and Murph

Courtney & Carson Kern

Murph, Mike Gatens and Louise

Bill & Ann came from Alaska

it's great to be a Hawkeye

Our friends and family surprised Louise and I by establishing an Iowa athletic scholarship in our names. Here is a copy of the letter.

4/20/2009

John and Bonnie Murphy
2218 Holiday Rd
Coralville, IA 52241

Dear John and Bonnie:

In the fall of 1950, Earle Murphy asked Louise Barnes out on their first date. He took her to a City High football game. It was a sign of things to come and since that first date Earle has escorted Louise to over one thousand sporting events and only about three movies!

During the past fifty years, Earle and Louise have become one of the foremost couples in Hawkeye history. They are loyal and positive fans who have done a great deal to promote the "Hawkeye Family" atmosphere at the University of Iowa. As owners of Bremers Men's Store in downtown Iowa City, Earle and Louise established numerous friendships with Iowa coaches, players, administrators, and fellow Hawkeye fans.

Our wish is to honor Earle and Louise by establishing the University of Iowa Earle and Louise Murphy Athletic Scholarship. The initial response to this concept has been very positive, and has encouraged us to proceed on behalf of their friends and family. Contributions qualify as a charitable gift, however they do not count toward annual I-Club recognition levels. True to "Murphy's Law", we realize these are challenging times, so pledges may be spread over a period of up to five years. Our initial goal is $50,000, which will endow a non-sport-specific scholarship. Our long range goal is $200,000, which will endow an Iowa Football scholarship.

Would you please consider joining us with a contribution to honor Earle and Louise. *As of now, this is a surprise to Earle and Louise.* We encourage you to submit your gift or pledge by August 1st, 2009. A pledge form and return envelope are enclosed. All donors will be invited to a celebration party to be held on an Iowa Football weekend this year. Specific questions can be directed to John Murphy at 319-936-3183 or e-mail jhnmurphy@qwestoffice.net.

It's great to be a Hawkeye. On Iowa! Go Hawks!

Sincerely,

C.W. "Bump" Elliott
UI Director of Athletics,
Emeritus

Darrell Wyrick
UI Foundation President,
Emeritus

John Murphy
On behalf of Ann,
Jim, Joe, Jeff, Jerry,
Mary Sue and our families

The University of Iowa
Earle and Louise Murphy Athletic Scholarship

Earle and Louise Murphy's involvement with Iowa Athletics:

- Earle Murphy is a life-long Iowa Hawkeye fan attending sporting events for over 70 years. Louise is an avid fan as well, and has supported and assisted Earle in all of his endeavors.
- Earle is a founding board member of the Johnson County I-Club and was President in 1974. The National I-Club selected Earle the "Hawk of the Year" in 1975. The Iowa Varsity Club named him an honorary "Letterman" in 1984.
- Earle was the driving force in bringing "The Hawk" sculpture to campus. Located between Carver Hawkeye Arena and Duane Banks Field, the sculpture is a symbol of Hawkeye spirit, and it honors the career of C.W. "Bump" Elliott.
- Earle was instrumental in opening the Amana VIP golf event to the public, with ticket proceeds benefiting Iowa athletics.
- Earle was a member of the former "Town Hawk" group. Earle and Louise befriended and counseled numerous Iowa football players including John Alt, Andre Tippett, Sam Palladino, and Norman Granger.
- Earle is "President for Life" of the "Garden Club", a lunch group of 65 devoted Hawkeye friends and fans who meet the Friday before every Iowa home football game. Louise is the gracious hostess.
- Earle is the founder and co-host of "Sports Opinion", a long-running local cable TV talk show which promotes Iowa Hawkeye and local sports.
- Earle and Louise have only missed a few of the Johnson County I-Club Friday morning breakfasts since he helped launch the tradition 35 years ago.
- In 1934, an eleven year old Earle Murphy was fighting polio. Hawkeye legend Ozzie Simmons befriended Earle and would carry him to Kelly Field (the old armory), where he would hike footballs to Ozzie and his friends. This helped forge his bond with and love of Hawkeye athletics.
- Willard "Sandy" Boyd, University of Iowa President Emeritus, wrote the following in a letter to Earle, "Your town and your university are indebted to you for 53 years of outstanding service as a friend to all thru Bremers and thru your many civic activities. Like Old Capitol, you are a great Iowa institution."
- Sportswriter Al Grady proclaimed that Earle was a "Hawk for all seasons" due to his enthusiastic support and attendance at numerous Iowa sporting events and booster activities. Al Grady also wrote, "If there is a more ardent booster, faithful follower, or dependable contributor to the Hawkeye cause than "Murph", he would be hard to find."

There are thousands of great Hawkeye fans.

Let's honor two of the best fans ever…forever.

Murph Remembers...

Friends & Family at the scholarship reception.   Photos courtesy of Bob Goodfellow

Photos courtesy of Bob Goodfellow

Top Row L-R: Jerry Murphy, John Murphy, Ann Murphy Pearson, Mary Sure Kern,
Joyce Barnes, Wayne Barnes and Mindy Krause
Bottom Row L-R: Jim Murphy, Lucile Kinney, Murph, Louise, Jeff Murphy and Joe Murphy

A few steps ahead of a pack of Wolverines. Tony Moeaki runs for a touchdown against Michigan on October 10, 2009

Photo Courtesy of Bob Goodfellow

Jets fly "Low and Fast" over Kinnick Stadium

The pre-game flyover before the Ohio State game on November 20, 2010, was exhilarating! I was sitting high in the outdoor club seats, and it seemed like the planes were at almost eye level. The four jets cleared the scoreboard by only 58 feet, and were at an altitude of just 16 feet above the press box. The jets also approached

Photo Courtesy of Bob Goodfellow

speeds of 400 knots, more than the required limit of 300 knots. The pilots of the four Talon T-38 jets were all disciplined for flying too low and too fast. It was a fun sight to witness.

"What My Children Remember..."

Jim Murphy ~
I remember a football player and his wife that took care of us when mom and dad were on a trip. We had to train the football player how to talk with us at dinnertime. He would say, "Is that ketchup?" and we would reply, "Yes". He expected us to offer it to him but no one offered ketchup until he requested, "May I have the ketchup, please?" I guess we liked playing word games.

Jeff Murphy ~
My favorite memory with dad is Iowa basketball games at the old Fieldhouse. I loved watching the games and feeling the excitement in the building. People were stomping their feet on the metal bleachers. We sat in the top row of the lower section. I grew up watching the great basketball teams of the 70's.

Ann Murphy Pearson ~
I agree with Jeff, I really liked going to the old Fieldhouse for basketball games. But, I remember how wrestling meets would pack the crowds in too. I loved watching wrestling matches. I remember watching this huge... probably 500-pound heavyweight wrestler from Iowa State come on the mat and proceed to squash his opponent. I was amazed that anyone would have the nerve to go up against him.

Jim Murphy ~
I remember attending a football game years ago. Dad and I were at Purdue and it was raining. Back in the old days you could bring umbrellas into the stadium. The man sitting in front of me had an umbrella. One of the endpoints touched my face and Dad told the guy to hold his umbrella up higher so that it wouldn't hit me. Well, it happened again. This time Dad is mad and tells the guy not to let it happen again. Shortly, the man isn't paying attention and lets the umbrella go back down and the point of the umbrella just about hits me in the eye. This time Dad doesn't give the umbrella man another warning. Dad just stands up and grabs the umbrella and in a split second he has snapped the umbrella in half and returned the two pieces to the owner. No one said a word for a while. I remember this incident freaked me out because I had never thought of dad as a tough guy. But that day, protecting me, I think he would have hurt that guy if he had even mentioned the broken umbrella.

Mary Sue Kern~
Mom and I would spend Sunday afternoons during football season making potato salad and deviled eggs for the coaches. We would cook dozens of eggs! Dad would take it over on Monday morning so the football staff would have something homemade to go with their sandwiches for lunch. The coaches really appreciated the food... they ate while they reviewed game film and discussed strategy for the next game.

John Murphy ~
Iowa Advances to the Final Four
Iowa had a great basketball team in 1980 with guard Ronnie Lester leading the team. I was a senior at Iowa and invited several college friends over to Mom and Dad's house to watch the Iowa vs. Georgetown basketball game. The winner would advance to play in the NCAA Final Four.

We were behind by 10 points in the second half and then rallied in the closing minutes. I had played percussion in the UI concert and marching bands, and during a commercial got on my drum set and played some Iowa drum cadences. Everyone was pumped up, excited and nervous. In the final seconds Steve Waite made a basket and free throw and we won 81-80 to win the game! All of us, including Mom and Dad, were jumping around and going crazy.

Right after the game, my college buddies and I drove downtown and the streets were filled with cars honking their horns and students cheering loudly. It was crazy how quickly everyone came downtown to celebrate the last minute victory and the realization that the Hawks were going to play in the Final Four! Later that night, the Fieldhouse arena was opened to fans to welcome the basketball team back to Iowa City. The Iowa wrestling team had just won a championship and about 10,000 excited Hawkeye fans attended the impromptu pep rally in the Fieldhouse. Lute Olson, Dan Gable and a few players addressed the crowd.

It was an incredible day in Hawkeye history, and one that Mom, Dad, and I still remember vividly. Go Hawks!

Ann Murphy Pearson ~

I remember the Homecoming Parties in the 1960's and 1970's we hosted at home on Ridge Road. We would make food all week, especially potato salad and deviled eggs. Everything had to be cleaned and organized... dad always wanted the house to look perfect. And that meant both inside and outside. Homecoming games always seemed to coincide with the leaves falling and that meant the Murphy kids would be out raking the yard while listening to the game on the radio. The yard needed to be leaf-free, just as dad had ordered. It would be beautiful. And do you know what would happen? Dad would come home and say, "Ann, close the curtains." So, I guess I just knew we had all done a good job and that the yard looked great even if the guest didn't see it.

The Murphy Boys ~

When mom and dad went on business trips like to New York City or Chicago to meet with vendors or to Japan to learn about a clothing line we often had football players and their wives take care of us. We all fondly remember the time that Linda and Roy Bash, an Iowa quarterback, moved into Ridge Road. Jeff remembers that Roy would have some of his fellow football players come over too. They taught us how to play the game, Rock, Paper, and Scissors. When someone lost they would hold their arm out, palm up. The winner would take two fingers and hit the loser on the wrist. Jeff's wrists were sore, but he had a great time.

Roy and Linda were very attentive and endearing and really did a great job of taking care of our big family.

Ann Murphy Pearson ~

When I was a senior in high school and had a boyfriend, dad realized that some day his children would probably get married. Weddings usually take place on Saturdays. And Saturdays are also when football games happen. So, one day during supper, he announced that no one should plan a wedding during the football season... at least if you wanted him at the wedding. I remember how funny that edict sounded at the time. But, I was married in March. Jeff, Jerry and Mary Sue were all married in the summer months. I guess we had all listened to him.

And 12 years ago John and Bonnie were discussing when they should have their wedding. The conversation was happening in May. My son, Bill, had just graduated from the University of Iowa's College of Law. I mentioned that if the wedding was the same weekend as an Iowa game it would be a double-header for me... football and family!

Well, I watched Bonnie's body language as she processed sharing her wedding day with Iowa football. She may be a true Hawkeye fan, but my request might have been asking too much. A couple days later the ideal decision was made... Saturday, September 20th, 2003 Iowa was scheduled to host Arizona State at home. John and Bonnie would be married on Friday evening and everyone could go to the game the next day. So, a wedding was held on Ridge Road and then the honeymoon started at Kinnick! And the Hawkeyes even gave them a wedding gift, an Iowa victory. I guess Dad's edict was rescinded, because he attended the wedding, held during football season and had a great time.

Joe Murphy ~

One of the biggest things in my life was realizing that Earle would be there for us if there was an event that we were competing in or a part of. Being one of the worst wrestlers to roll thru the halls of Central Junior High, I was surprised to look over and see my father in the stands cheering for me. It was easy to see him because most of the time I was on my back fighting for a few more seconds of time on the mat. He would leave the store and make it to our events and was there for us even when it was not easy for him.

How much he supported us was shown to me one Sunday when I wanted to go race my motorcycle in Tipton, Iowa. I was sulking around on Saturday because I did not have a way to get there. Sunday morning comes early and Dad is yelling at me to get up and get with it. He had gone and picked up the Bremers company van, and we loaded up and went racing. Did I mention that Earle hated motorcycles? Race tracks at that time were not too special. No spectator seating, outhouses and lots of dust and heat. I don't remember how I finished that day but dad took his only day off and spent it on me. That made him the winner.

Jerry Murphy ~

It was a Saturday in the mid 1970's and Dad and I were in the back yard raking leaves. We were also listening to an away Iowa football game on the radio. It was one of a few road games during the Bob Commings era that Dad didn't attend. Iowa was getting beat pretty bad and Dad was getting very frustrated. I said, "Dad, it's only a game." Dad responded, "I know, but it's IOWA."

"The Swarm"
Here Come The Hawkeyes!

Murph Remembers...

Murph and Pat Foster

Decade Ten | 2013-2016

Decade 10 — "Murph remembers..."

John Streif - The most compassionate, kind, and selfless Hawkeye

John was an athletic trainer at Iowa for 40 years, retiring in 2012. He also coordinated the travel plans for the football and men's basketball teams. As a trainer, the care and compassion he administered to athletes dealing with injuries is legendary.

For decades, when we attended a year end basketball banquet, it seemed like most of the comments and praise from the senior athletes would be directed toward John Streif. You could tell by the emotion in their voices, how much they truly admired him.

Due to a financial gift from former Hawkeye basketball star Ronnie Lester, the new training facilities at Carver-Hawkeye arena were named in his honor. Besides numerous professional awards, John was co-recipient of the Chris Street award in 1997, and Kirk Ferentz presented him with the game ball following Iowa's 19-16 win in the 2001 Alamo Bowl.

An example of his selflessness happened recently. On September 18th, 2015, there was a reunion in Iowa City with Lute Olson and several of his former players and staff. They all toured Carver-Hawkeye Arena, and had dinner at Fran & Margaret McCaffery's house. They attended the Iowa football game at Kinnick Stadium, where the Hawks beat Pittsburgh with a 57-yard field goal on the final play of the game. As much as John would have loved to be at all these events, he decided to represent the U of I and drive to Michigan to attend the funeral of Roy Marble, Iowa's all time leading scorer in basketball.

I'm currently living in the Briarwood Care Center in Iowa City. John visits and usually drops off a Daily Iowan newspaper. I know he spreads his kindness and compassion on a daily basis in care centers and hospitals throughout the Iowa City community.

"Smiley"

If you've spent any time in downtown Iowa City, or at a local sporting event, you may have met or seen Gary Bloore. Gary is primarily known by his nickname, "Smiley." His nickname fits him, as he is always smiling and happy. He's a huge sports fan, and often attends area athletic events. He especially likes high school and college softball. His next favorite sports are football and basketball. "Smiley" says Dan Gable and Gayle Blevins are two of the best coaches ever at Iowa.

'Smiley" retired on May 13th, 2016, after working 44 years for the University of Iowa. He moved from his family farm in Elwood, IA for a job as a dishwasher at the UI Oakdale campus. He lived and worked there for 10 years before moving to Iowa City to perform the same job at Currier Hall. He's also worked at Hillcrest and most recently Burge Hall. He's washed a lot of dishes, and he's looking forward to retirement. With his extra time he plans on attending even more sporting events. He also loves going to concerts, and he's seen Carrie Underwood four times.

When I would go to an out of town Iowa football game, I'd bring a program back for "Smiley". He would also come into the store to buy badges we sold for home games. He always carried a paper grocery bag full of photos he'd taken of Iowa coeds. He has badges made with photos of his favorite athletes and Miss Iowa beauty queens attached to his shirt. Also, Smiley always wears a cap embroidered with the name of one of his favorite athletes.

Smiley is a regular customer at the Hamburg Inn, George's Buffet, and the Airliner. He still enjoys meeting and socializing with college students, and he's still not afraid to hitchhike to attend sporting events and concerts. I've always enjoy seeing "Smiley" around town. After talking to him, he always ends the conversation with, "It was nice to see you." He's a very special and admired Iowa City icon. "Smiley" is a loyal, positive, friendly, and smiling Hawkeye!

Mark Wilson
Hawkeye Memorabilia Collector and Historian

Mark Wilson has a passion for Iowa athletics and Hawkeye history. As an ambassador at the UI Athletics Hall of Fame and Museum, Mark loves being around the memorabilia and trophies, and educating visitors about historic Hawkeye events. And when he returns home, he's still able to revisit many of his own Hawkeye memories in a room he calls the Hawks Nest.

In a 40-by-13 foot room in his basement, Mark has one of the finest Iowa memorablia collections I've seen. It includes more than 200 framed items, including large displays featuring Nile Kinnick, Forest Evashevski, and Hayden Fry. Mark has numerous autographed footballs, basketballs, game programs, and a complete set of Iowa homecoming buttons. The most he's paid for one item was $450.00 for a 1943 homecoming button made of paper. It was made of paper because metal was needed for the war effort.

An autographed football is one of Mark's finest and most unique items. It contains 59 signatures dating back to athletes who played for Iowa eight decades ago. From Ironman Red Frye, who played in 1939, to current NFL player and former Hawkeye Chad Greenway, the football is loaded with famous autographs. Other signatures include Forest Evashevski, Randy Duncan, Ken Ploen, Bob Jeter, Willie Fleming, Alex Karras, John Niland, Ed Podolak, Andre Tippett, Chuck Long, Marv Cook, Bump Elliott, Hayden Fry, Kirk Ferentz, Tim Dwight, Tavian Banks, Nate Kaeding, Bob Sanders, Robert Gallery, and many more...and of course, it's a work in progress.

Mark Wilson, proudly standing in his Hawks Nest room. He has more than 250 framed, unique Hawkeye items.

Homecoming button collection

In front of his Nile Kinnick wall with his football autographed by numerous Hawkeyes.

Mark's quilt made from 27 Hawkeye t-shirts

Murph Remembers...

Ted Pacha
Mr. "I-Club"

His license plates simply state I CLUB, an organization that Ted's been involved with locally since 1975. Ted's past President of both the Johnson County I-Club and National I-Club. During a local I-Club membership drive in 1975, Ted signed up 50 new members, and followed that up by recruiting 100 new members the next year. In 1999, Ted was honored by the UI Varsity Club as an Honorary Letterman.

Ted founded Hawkeye Medical Supply, a business he grew from an idea to employing better than 100 employees. He was co-owner of Duffy's Collectible Cars for ten years. Ted generously supports Regina High School and University of Iowa athletics. Enjoy these photos of Ted's amazing collection of Hawkeye memorabilia and antique cars.

Entrance to Ted's Hawkeye Room.

Ted standing next to his "Corvette Mechanic Herky."

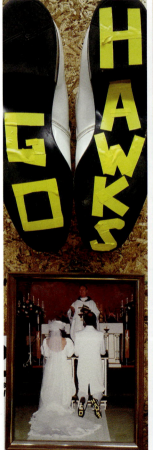

Ted says "I do and Go Hawks!"

An old item in his collection I really like. A megaphone, compliments of Bremers, with the 1926 football and basketball schedules.

Ted has more than 18,000 Hawkeye related badges, including two complete sets of Homecoming buttons.

Ted Pacha loves his Hawkeyes, and his cars too!

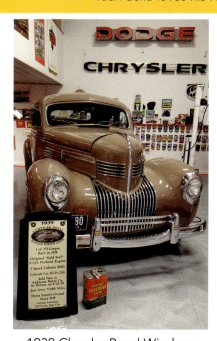

1939 Chrysler Royal Windsor Business Coupe

Dodge Viper Collection

Wow…and this is just a portion of Ted's collection of more than 40 antique cars.

Chevrolet Corvette Collection

Fun at Football Games

On September 11, 1993 we played Iowa State at Jack Trice stadium. It was my birthday. John had arranged for a plane to fly a banner around the stadium three times. It was really windy and the plane struggled and flew slowly one direction. It was pushed by the wind and flew quickly on the way back. The Hawks gave me a present too. We beat Iowa State 31-28.

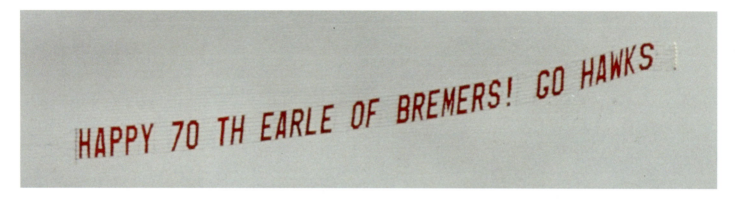

I really like it when my family gets together to go to Iowa events. The Alaskan group came for Thanksgiving and the Iowa-Nebraska game. We had enough black and gold to outfit everyone.

Ann & Roger Pearson, Bill & Becky Pearson, Louise & Murph
Ready for the Iowa-Nebraska game on November 25, 2012. It was cold!

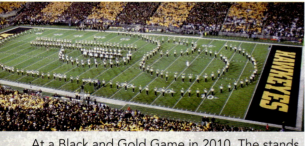

At a Black and Gold Game in 2010. The stands looked great with the alternating Hawkeye stripes. It was Homecoming and we beat Penn State 24-3.

The IOWA banners take a run around the stadium after Iowa scores!
GO HAWKS!

Iowa Hawkeye Friends

There's John and Murph but where's Louise?

With June & Mike Kinney. We beat LSU on the final play! Capital One Bowl Game in 2005.

Louise, Hayden Fry, Murph after riding together at FRY fest

Earle and Louise Murphy
Iowa City Press Citizen Photo
1976

My #1 Hawkeye
My wife Louise!

With former Bremers employee Mark Walz

Murph Remembers...

"Goody"

Doug "Goody" Goodfellow is a great Hawkeye fan and one of Bump Elliott's best friends. Goody would stop by the store in the mornings to visit and have a cup of coffee. After leaving Bremers he'd go to Carver-Hawkeye arena and visit with Bump and other athletic department administrators and coaches. I doubt there is anyone who's not a UI employee, who has spent more time with UI coaches and administrators than Goody. If he ever decides to write a book, it's one I'd love to read.

"Goody" owned Goodfellow Printing in Iowa City from 1955-1995, and his sons Bob and Brad now manage the company. They have published and sold the home game programs for men's and women's basketball games for many years. They also coordinate selling the football programs at Kinnick Stadium.

"Goody" has spent more than 48 years assisting the Iowa athletic department. Since 1968, he has been the public address spotter for home football and basketball games. He's done the same job for home wrestling meets since 1974. He says he keeps doing it because he has the best seat in the house. "Goody" has worked with Father Bob Holzhammer and Mark Kamps in basketball, Bud Suter, Frosty Mitchell, Father Bob Holzhammer, and Mark Abbott in football, and Phil Haddy in wrestling.

"Goody" was a volunteer assistant coach with the Iowa golf team for many years, working with head coaches Chuck Zweiner, Lynn Blevins, and Terry Anderson. He organized practice schedules and travel plans for the golf teams. He was someone the players could talk to about their school and golf team issues. Some of the elite Hawkeye golfers during his tenure were Lonnie Nielsen, Dave Rummells, Guy Boros, Brad Klapprott, and Sean McCarty.

With "Goody" having spent so much time at athletic events, he has some great stories.

One of my favorites dates back to the mid 1970's. Larry Coyer was an assistant coach with Bob Commings in football, and Dan Gable was an assistant coach with Gary Kurdelmeier in wrestling. Phil Haddy worked in the UI Sports Information Department and was also the public address announcer for home wrestling meets. Coyer had remarked to Haddy that he'd recently worked out with Gable and "held his own." During a break in the action at a wrestling meet, Phil Haddy announced to the crowd, "In other sports news, Larry Coyer wrestled Dan Gable, with Coyer winning 2-1. Haddy was kidding but Gable wasn't laughing. The next day after their workout, Coyer told Haddy that Gable absolutely "beat the crap out of me."

Doug "Goody" Goodfellow has devoted a lot of time and energy to Iowa athletics. He's a nice guy, one of my best friends, and truly a good fellow!

L to R: Doug Goodfellow, Bruce Pearl, Tim Doherty, Duane Banks, Mark Jennings

Pictured left to right: Gil Barker, seated in striped referee shirt, PA announcer Father Bob Holzhammer, and Doug Goodfellow working during a basketball game in the Iowa Field House.

Photo Courtesy of Bob Goodfellow
George Raveling having fun with Goody

Goody checking out Tiger Woods during a college tournament

Earle and Louise Murphy and Doug and Marge Goodfellow
Celebrating The Goodfellows' 60th wedding anniversary

Megan Blank
Iowa Softball Superstar with a Bremers family history

Louise and I were excited when it was announced that Megan Blank accepted a University of Iowa softball scholarship. Her parents, Jim and Marcia, met while working for us. Jim worked as a salesman and manager at Bremers, and Marcia worked at our Zipper jean stores.

We closely followed Megan's Iowa career, which spanned from 2012 thru 2015. Jim told me Megan was pretty talented, and I was eager to see how much playing time she would get during her career. Well, the first game of her freshman year she started at shortstop, and then proceeded to start in all 213 games during her four years at Iowa.

Megan had a great career and set several records. Her batting average was .442 her senior season, and .410 for her career, both Iowa records. She finished her career first in career doubles, second all-time in RBIs, fourth in home runs, and fifth in runs scored. Megan was named First Team All-Big Ten in 2015.

We really enjoyed attending her Senior Day game victory against Northwestern. Afterwards, we got to congratulate Megan on her great career, and visit with the entire Blank family.

Enjoying Megan Blank's senior day
Front L to R: Earle and Louise
Back L to R: Marcia, JD, Jim, and Megan Blank

Wrestling at Kinnick

On Saturday, November 14, 2015, more than 112,000 fans watched wrestling and football at historic Kinnick Stadium.

During the early afternoon, 42,287 fans watched the Iowa wrestlers beat #1 ranked Oklahoma State 18-16. The wrestling meet shattered the previous NCAA attendance record of 15,996 set by Penn State in 2013.

Later that evening, 70,585 fans watched the Iowa football team beat Minnesota 40-35, to achieve a 10-0 record for the first time ever in a single season. In addition, it was great to reclaim possession of our favorite pig, the "Floyd of Rosedale" trophy.

What an amazing, historic, and beautiful day to be a Hawkeye. Our fans are the best in the country!

Murph Remembers...

Iowa Coaches and Administrators
Stability...Consistency...Longevity

There are several examples throughout the UI athletic department that demonstrate long term continuity. I believe it's due to the fact that the University of Iowa is a great place to work, and the Iowa City area is a great place to live. The fact that we've only had three athletic directors the last 47 years has helped with less transition.

Our athletic department is self supported, and does not receive money from the State of Iowa. All expenses, including student athlete scholarships, are funded primarily by ticket sales, television revenue, and donations from our great fans. I'm proud of this fact.

Of course, sometimes you need to make changes, but I think we've been very fortunate with the quality of coaches and key staff hired and retained by our last three athletic directors. *I've put together a few examples to illustrate this point, focusing on the people, sports, and jobs with which I'm most familiar. I hope this partial list of names and dates brings back memories for you as well.*

Only three Athletic Directors the last 47 years.

- **Director of Athletics:** Bump Elliott 1970-1991, Bob Bowlsby 1991-2006, Gary Barta 2006 to present.

   Executive Secretary: Rae Parker 1986 to present.
   Bob Bowlsby is currently the Commissioner of the Big 12 Conference

Only two Head Football coaches the last 38 years.

- **Football Coaches:** Frank Lauterbur 1971-1973, Bob Commings 1974-1978
   Hayden Fry 1979-1998, Kirk Ferentz 1999 to present.

   Head Coach Secretary: Rita Foley 1978 to present
   Secretary: Deb Abbott and Amy Thomas

Illinois, Indiana, and Minnesota each had eight head coaches during the same time period.
It also takes talented and loyal assistant coaches to run a successful program. Hayden and Kirk have both done great jobs of hiring and retaining quality assistants.

- **Women's Athletic Director:** Christine Grant 1973-2000

- **Chief Financial Officers:** Francis "Buzz" Graham 1952-1980,
   Larry Bruner 1980-2002, Mick Walker 2002 to present.
   Mick has worked in UI business operations since 1982

- **Sports Information/ Communications Director:** George Wine 1968-1993, Phil Haddy 1993-2011,
   Steve Roe 2011 to present.
   Steve Roe has worked in UI athletic communications since 1990
   (Eric Wilson held the position from 1923-1968)

- **Director for Compliance:** Fred Mims 1985-2015
   Lyla Clerry 1985 to present

- **Athletic Fundraisers:** Mark Jennings 1987- present, Andy Piro 1989 to present,
   Matt Henderson 1994 to present

- **Wrestling Coaches:** Dave McCuskey 1953-1972, Gary Kurdelmeier 1972-1976,
   Dan Gable 1976-1997, Jim Zalesky 1997-2006,
   Tom Brands 2006 to present
   Secretary: Helen Hohle and Judy Leonard

- **Baseball Coaches:** Duane Banks 1971-1997, Scott Broghamer 1998-2003,
   Jack Dahm 2004-2013, Rick Heller 2014 to present

- **Basketball Coaches: (Men's)** Lute Olson 1974-1983, George Raveling 1983-1986, Tom Davis 1986-1999, Steve Alford 1999-2007 Todd Lickliter 2007-2010, Fran McCaffery 2010 to present
Director of Operations: Jerry Strom 1981-2013   Secretary: Shelly Deutsch

- **Basketball Coaches: (Women's)** Lark Birdsong 1974-1979, Judy McMullen 1979-1983, C. Vivian Stringer 1983-1995, Angie Lee 1995-2000, Lisa Bluder 2000 to present

- **Tennis Coaches:** Don Klotz 1948-1968, John Winnie 1969-1981, Steve Houghton 1982-2014, Ross Wilson 2014 to present

- **Cross Country and Track Coaches:** Francis Cretzmeyer 1948-1978, Ted Wheeler 1978-1997 Larry Wieczorek 1987-2014, Layne Anderson 2012 to present, and Joey Woody 2014 to present

- **Gymnastic Coaches:** Dick Holzaepfel 1950-1966 and 1971-1980, Tom Dunn 1981-2010, JD Reive 2010 to present

- **Swimming & Diving Coaches:** Robert Allen 1959-1975, Glenn Patton 1976-1999, Bob Rydze 1977-2012, John Davey 1999-2004 Marc Long 2004 to present

(Dave Armbruster coached swimming at Iowa from 1917-1958. He created and developed the "butterfly stroke," with the assistance of UI swimmer Jack Sieg)

- **Golf Coaches: (Men's)** Chuck Zwiener 1958-1990, Lynn Blevins 1990-1993, Terry Anderson 1994-2007, Mark Hankins 2007-2014 Tyler Stith 2014 to present

- **Golf Coaches: (Women's)** Diane Thomason 1975-2002, Bobbie Carney 2003-2006 Kelly Crawford 2006-2011, Megan Menzel 2011 to present

- **Softball Coaches:** Jane Hagedorn 1974-1980, Ginny Parrish 1980-1987 Gayle Blevins 1988-2010, Marla Looper 2011 to present

Other past and present athletic department staff I'd like to acknowledge:

Athletic Relations: Bud Suter   **Legal:** Mark Abbott   **Varsity Club:** Les Steenlage
Human Resources: Mary Curtis and Lori Neu   **Event Management:** Paula Jantz
Ticket Managers: Jean Kupka, Mike Naughton, and Pam Finke
Ticket Office: Marilyn Stagg and Donna Howe
Team Physicians: Dr. Shorty Paul, Dr. John Albright, Dr. Harley Feldick, Dr. David Johnston, Dr. Ned Amendola, and Dr. Brian Wolf
Athletic Trainers: Tom Spalj, Arnie Buntrock, Ed Crowley, John Streif, Dan Foster, Russ Haynes, and Mike Lawler
Fundraisers: Howard Vernon, Jersey Jermier, Dan McDonald, and Bud Callahan
Equipment Managers: Ron Fairchild, Doug Garrett, Greg Morris, and Kevin Foor
Finkbine golf course and athletic grounds maintenance: Ted Thorn and Mike Hoffman
Finkbine Secretary: Kris Stumpf
Video Production: Mike Moriarity, Matt Engelbert, and Jerry Palmer
Hall of Fame/Licensing: Dale Arens   **Secretary:** Christa Roberts
Marketing and External Relations: Rick Klatt and Mary Jo Kinney
Academic Counselor: Bill Munn   **Sports Pyschologist:** Gene Gauron
Sports Counselor: Marvin Sims, Sr   **Facilities:** Del Gehrke and Damian Simcox

There are many people that did not get acknowledged who have and continue to work for the betterment of UI Athletics. Thanks to all who have made my Hawkeye fan experience so enjoyable.

I like the slogan Gary Barta uses: "Win. Graduate. Do it Right."
It's Great to be a Hawkeye!

"Win. Graduate. Do it Right."

Bob Brooks
Radio broadcaster for over 72 years

Bob Brooks has a great radio voice, and evidently a great work ethic. He's worked in radio broadcasting for an amazing 72 years, starting at age 17 in 1943. At the age of 89, Bob covered the 2016 Rose Bowl. The press box at Kingston Stadium in Cedar Rapids is named in his honor. Bob was inducted into the College Football Hall of Fame in 2004.

Last fall I was in the Kinnick Stadium press box during a football game. I struck up a conversation with two women who were wearing red sport coats. They were Rose Bowl representatives and were at the game to check out our team and our fans. I introduced them to my wife Louise, who was born in Pasadena, California. Bob Brooks stopped by to visit and I told him about the Rose Bowl reps. He quickly went to work asking them numerous questions.

Bob is beloved by Hawkeye fans. He's famous for still using his old fashioned, large tape recorder at press conferences and for interviews. He's a great guy.

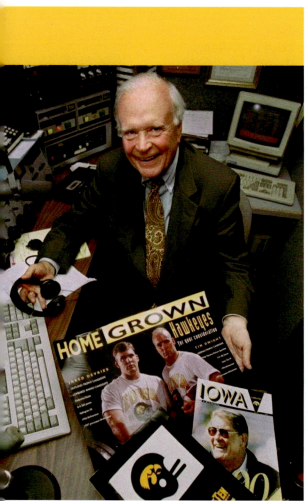

Bob Brooks, over 72 years in radio broadcasting… a Hawkeye legend.
Des Moines Register photo

Zach Johnson being interviewed by Bob Brooks

Fred Mims - Iowa administrator and baseball star

Fred Mims recently retired after a 38-year career with the UI Athletics Department. He was an associate athletics director with duties that included running the Office of Athletics Student Services. His department dealt with compliance, financial aid, eligibility, and graduation rates.

Fred also assumed administrative responsibility for the sports of wrestling and baseball. He was involved on the process of hiring current wrestling coach Tom Brands, and current baseball coach Rick Heller.

I remember watching Fred play baseball for Iowa. He was big and strong, and a great power hitter. Fred was a two-time first team all-Big Ten selection.

I attended the Big Ten championship game in 1972. Fred hit two home runs, leading the Hawks to a victory over Northwestern. The Hawkeyes stayed hot in the post season, and made it all the way to the College World Series.

Decade Ten | 2013-2016 155

Earle and Louise Murphy renewed their wedding vows after 64 years of marriage during a ceremony held at Briarwood Health Care Center. (Iowa City Press Citizen photo)

"I can't wait till football Saturdays!"

Patriotic Herky
Showing the Hawkeye spirit for the USA

I Just Love Iowa Football

A Black and Gold night game

Visiting with Spirit Squad girls
Riding with Tim Dwight
Watching a game
Louise and Murph at Kinnick
Ann and Murph cheering
Tailgating with Mike Kinney after a game

An Epic Birthday

I didn't realize it, but during the broadcast of the Iowa-Missouri State game on September 7, 2013, Gary Dolphin and Eddie Podolak talked about my upcoming birthday. They encouraged any listeners who knew me to send me birthday cards. And people listened! I got mail for weeks! It was great to have so many friends remember me and send me good wishes.

Ode to Earle
There once was a fine gent named Earle,
Who used to have lots of red curls.
Some hair may be gone,
But his spirit's still strong.
And to his friends he's a real pearl!

Written by Ann Murphy Pearson for my 90th

Murph and Louise at his 90th birthday celebration
September 11, 2013

Tailgating with John and Bonnie Murphy.
Awaiting the pre-game champagne toast given by Ed Otten.
Go Hawks!

Tailgating with Chuck Long

The 91st Birthday Sign at Kinnick

I attended the Iowa- Iowa State game on September 13, 2014, the weekend after my 91st birthday. My daughter Ann accompanied me to the game. We spent time tailgating before the game and drove around looking at all of the different ways Hawkeye fans celebrate.

Once we were in Kinnick Stadium, Ann was really interested in the messages being displayed on the Jumbotron. During the timeouts we would read about different folks celebrating birthdays and anniversaries. During one break she pointed at the Jumbotron sign and yelled, "Dad, this message is for YOU!"

I looked up and sure enough the sign was showing a message wishing me a Happy 91st birthday. My children had arranged this and it was fun to see my name in lights at Kinnick!

Kirk Ferentz

Kirk Ferentz is first and foremost, a great person. He would be successful in whatever career he chose. Kirk is smart, kind, detail oriented, honest, and humble. His assistant coaches love working with him. Kirk and his staff do a great job preparing Iowa players for professional football, and more importantly, for life beyond football.

Kirk and his wife Mary have made generous contributions to the UI College of Liberal Arts. Also, Mary organizes the Iowa Women's Football Academy, a yearly event which has raised more than one million dollars for the University of Iowa Children's Hospital.

The recent 2015 football season was one of the best ever. It was exciting, as we won our first 12 games, and claimed the Big Ten West Division title. We finished with a 12-2 overall record, losing to Stanford in the Rose Bowl. The 12 wins in one season was a record for a Hawkeye football team. Iowa won all four trophy games with wins over Iowa State, Wisconsin, Minnesota, and Nebraska. We also added the Big Ten West Division trophy, so we now possess five trophies from the 2015 season.

Kirk Ferentz was named the 2015 Big Ten Coach of the Year. Kirk is now a four-time Big Ten Coach of the Year recipient. He won numerous national honors for the 2015 season, including the Eddie Robinson Coach of the Year, the Bobby Dodd Coach of the Year, and the Woody Hayes Coach of the Year awards.

The Bobby Dodd Coach of the Year Award honors the head coach whose program embodies the awards' three pillars of scholarship, leadership and integrity, while also having success on the playing field. It's a very prestigious honor and Kirk and his entire staff are deserving recipients.

Kirk currently has the longest tenure of any head coach in the Big Ten, and is tied for first in longevity among all BCS schools. I believe and hope that Kirk will someday join his predecessor, Hayden Fry, in the College Football Hall of Fame.

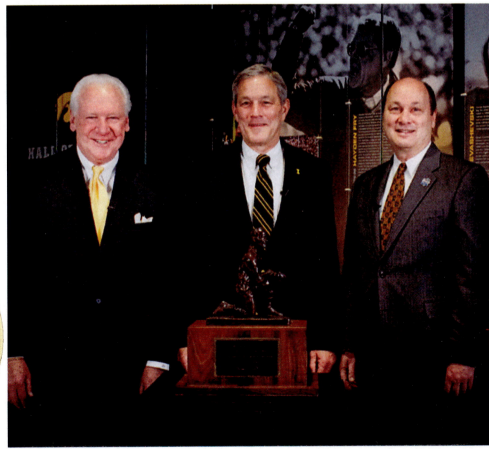

Kirk Ferentz going to work on Game Day

Photo Courtesy of UI Athletics Department

The New Football Facility is Fantastic

Photos Courtesy of UI Athletics Department

I was fortunate to be given a tour of the new football facility. Former assistant coach Bernie Wyatt showed me around the new offices, meeting rooms, locker rooms, weight room, indoor practice facility, and much more. It's one of the best in the country, and it's a great asset to our football program. I'm sure it will start paying dividends in recruiting and performance right away. Go Hawks!

God Bless Us, Everyone

I've had this Tiny Tim doll for a very long time. Of course, I relate to it since I've limped around most of my life, and used crutches for quite awhile.

It was first displayed in the Christmas window of Armstrong's Department Store. Bremers had its own window display artist, Norman Meyers, and he knew the window designer at Armstrong's. Norman asked if he could have the Tiny Tim doll, and then he gave it to me. Tiny Tim has been part of the Murphy Family Christmas tradition ever since.

In the Christmas Carol by Charles Dickens, Tiny Tim would say....
"God Bless Us, Everyone!"

I wish the same to all of you.

Santa (Tom Robinson) visits Murph in December 2014 as cardboard cutout Kirk keeps a watchful eye. Murph asks Santa for a perfect 12-0 regular season for 2015... and his wish came true.

Next Generation Hawkeye

Photo Courtesy of Ann Murphy Pearson

My great-grandson Samuel Earl, with the teddy bear I gave Ann on her first birthday.